Kristal Leebrick

DAYTON'S
A TWIN CITIES INSTITUTION

Charleston  London

THE
History
PRESS

Published by The History Press
Charleston, SC 29403
www.historypress.net

First published 2013

Manufactured in the United States

ISBN 978.1.60949.672.2

Library of Congress CIP data applied for.

Contents

CONTENTS

Foreword

Department stores once defined the places they served. In this era of online purchases, big-box stores and national franchises, where shopping has become more a matter of low cost and convenience than one of commerce among friends in a community, traditional department stores seem like twentieth-century holdovers, even though many still remain.

Sadly, Dayton's is not one of them. Its disappearance in the early twenty-first century, rebranded first as Marshall Field's and then as Macy's, represents not just the loss of a well-respected, nationally known retailer but also the demise of a business that, in many ways, defined Minnesota as a place.

As Kristal Leebrick's book, *Dayton's: A Twin Cities Institution*, makes clear, that department store and its namesake family gave as much to Minnesota as they received. The Dayton family built a company that attracted the loyalty of its staff as well as its customers and one that focused on quality goods and service that few of its competitors could match. The family also supported local arts and cultural institutions to an extraordinary extent, often without fanfare or even recognition.

The company also embraced change, even when that ultimately led to the department store's demise. It created the world's first enclosed suburban shopping mall, Southdale, and started the formula of having competing department stores—in this case, Donaldson's—terminating the ends of the mall. Dayton's also embraced discount retailing by starting Target, which outgrew its parent company and eventually divested itself of the department store division that gave it birth.

While that divestiture made sense from a business perspective, it represented one more example of how retailing has largely lost a sense of place and, with it, a loss of community support and customer loyalty. Some say that this is inevitable, that the global economy makes it too hard for regional department stores to compete with national chains and digital shopping.

But success in the global economy also stems from luring an increasingly mobile workforce to places that offer a high quality of life and a distinct identity. Dayton's helped give that to some of Minnesota's major cities and suburbs, and the recounting of its history here reminds us that the businesses that care about the places they serve will remain the ones we most remember.

Thomas Fisher
Dean of the College of Design at the University of Minnesota

Acknowledgments

I t takes a metropolitan area and then some to write about a department store that was part of the fabric of many people's lives here in Minnesota and beyond.

I could not have written the history of Dayton's department store without leaning heavily on the book *George Draper Dayton: A Man of Parts*, written by Bruce B. Dayton and Ellen B. Green. The privately published biography of Bruce Dayton's grandfather George Draper Dayton tells the story of the man who founded Dayton's, as well as that of the store's first thirty-five years. I pulled a lot of information from it. Thank you Bruce Dayton and Ellen Green. And thank you to my mother-in-law, Greta Stryker, for loaning me her copy of that book.

Sally Glassberg Sands, director of special events at Dayton's in the 1980s, put me in touch with Paul Campbell and Kathleen Campbell. Paul told me about his efforts in quickly crafting a study that helped the Dayton Hudson Corporation fight a 1987 hostile takeover, and Kathleen introduced me to Jean McElvain, assistant curator at the Goldstein Museum of Design at the University of Minnesota, and to Dolores DeFore, merchandising manager at Dayton's Oval Room before going to Harold with Robert Dayton. Thank you, Kathleen and Paul, for your time and expertise.

Jean McElvain and Eunice Haugen opened the Goldstein archives to me and enabled me to tell the story of Jeanne Auerbacher, the Oval Room Queen in the 1940s and 1950s. Eunice encouraged me to call Margot Siegel, Auerbacher's daughter, who is now living in Miami, Florida, and I'm glad I did.

Margot, a retired journalist and founder of Friends of the Goldstein, is a great storyteller. I wish I could have taken her up on a visit to Miami to look at her photographs and art and find out more about Twin Cities fashion and pop culture.

I can't thank Dolores DeFore—the woman who brought the London look to Minneapolis in the 1960s—enough for sitting down with me to talk about her days at Dayton's and working with Stuart Wells and in the Oval Room.

And to Jack Barkla and Dan Mackerman, whose eighth-floor artwork has delighted and inspired us all for decades—you two rock.

It took writing this book to get me inside the Hennepin History Museum, a charming brick mansion that sits catty-corner from the Minneapolis Institute of Arts on Third Avenue. The place is a treasure, and I thank Susan Larson-Fleming, James Bacigalupo, Sarah Bell and Pam Albinson for their help with my research.

Another Minneapolis treasure is the Minneapolis History Collection and Special Collections on the fourth floor of the Minneapolis Central Library. Resource librarians Bailey Diers and Gail Wolfson went above and beyond in helping me locate photographs and news clippings. They pulled out the Dayton's collection for me every time I asked.

Thomas Fisher, dean of the College of Design at the University of Minnesota, wrote the foreword to this book and gave some great insight into Southdale and the Dayton brothers who built it. He also put me in touch with Judy Dayton, wife of Kenneth Dayton. Judy must be one of the busiest octogenarians in Minnesota, and I am grateful that she found time to talk on the phone about her days with Madame Auerbacher in the fitting rooms at the Oval Room and more.

To Eric Dayton, grandson of Bruce Dayton and son of Minnesota governor Mark Dayton, I appreciate your time spent talking with me about George Draper Dayton's great-great-grandsons' foray into the retail world.

Thanks to Sarah Massey, Alice Duggan, Jan Sedgewick, Audrey Estebo, Tim Mehner, Leanne Dobson, Claudia Wielgorecki and Rose Gregoire, all of whom shared their personal Dayton's tales with me. I also give a shout-out to the folks at Micawber's Books, who put me up to this project, and to author Roger Bergerson, who helped me obtain the photos of the Curtiss airplanes and allowed me to borrow an anecdote from his book, *Winging It at a Country Crossroads.*

And last, to my friend and colleague Ruth Weleczki, who read the whole book before I sent it to the publisher: dinner at the Bachelor Farmer is on me.

Introduction

Alice Duggan was an art student at the University of Minnesota in 1963 when she bought a fine-cotton batiste nightgown from the lingerie department at Dayton's in downtown Minneapolis. "It was the prettiest nightgown I've ever owned," she said.

Visiting the Dayton's lingerie department was an elegant experience for Duggan, who had moved to Minnesota from a small Ohio town to attend college. "All the merchandise was behind the counter," she said. If you wanted to look at a piece of clothing, you told the saleswomen your size, "and they would open a little drawer and hand it to you. You didn't help yourself from racks as you do now."

The most dramatic display in the department was a locked glass showcase along one wall, Duggan said. "If you saw something behind the glass that you would like to look at or try on, you got a salesperson to unlock that case for you—and that's where you could [find] something really glamorous." Like Duggan's Iris-brand nightgown. Made of hand-embroidered cotton as fine as silk, "it was very, very lovely," she said.

Say "Dayton's" to people who lived in the Twin Cities any time before 2001, and they likely will have an anecdote about the store. Dayton's was the place where Minnesotans bought clothes designed by Norman Norell or Hattie Carnegie, as well as bargain pieces off the rack, appliances and stereos, lawn mowers and canoes, airline tickets for their first trip abroad and more. Dayton's was where you could buy a cashmere sweater for a song during an Anniversary Sale or one of pop artist Tom Wesselmann's *Great American Nudes* from Gallery 12 on the top floor.

Elizabeth Cecil Haas wears a Persian silk gown—made by Dayton's bridal department—at her wedding to Donald Gregoire in September 1947. The Gregoires' daughters, Rose and Nancy, each wore the dress in their own weddings in 1986 and 1992, respectively.

Dayton's was the job that put many Minnesotans through college or the career that took them to retirement.

Dayton's made the Persian silk gown that Elizabeth Cecil Haas wore at her wedding to Donald Gregoire in September 1947, the dress that both her daughters, Rose and Nancy, wore in their own weddings decades later.

Dayton's was the store that commissioned Jan Sedgewick to make by hand more than four hundred blush-pink China silk lampshades for the cosmetics departments in all of the store branches in 1980. Sixteen inches in diameter at the bottom, eight inches in diameter at the top and fifteen inches deep, the silk was folded into quarter-inch pleats. The shades sat on pink Lucite bases.

The project earned a nod in Barbara Flanagan's *Minneapolis Star* column at the time. The pink silk "was a nice color for light to come through," said Sedgewick, who enjoyed walking into the store with her sons and saying, "Mommy made those."

The history of Dayton's is as much the history of George Draper Dayton—who took a gamble on opening a store on an out-of-the-way block in Minneapolis at the beginning of the twentieth century—as it is the history of the people who worked there, shopped there or simply made an annual event of seeing the Christmas window displays that opened on Thanksgiving.

"It was a great store," said Judy Dayton, wife of Ken Dayton, one of the five brothers who took the company from a single department store in 1950 to a corporation that built the first enclosed shopping mall in 1956 and launched Target in 1962. "The five boys working together as closely as they did is really remarkable," she said.

The first-floor button in the Eighth Street parking garage elevator in downtown Minneapolis still says, "Dayton's."

11

Dayton's had an almost one-hundred-year run in Minnesota, and its absence is still felt by many. The building where it all started remains a department store, and the first-floor button in the Eighth Street parking garage elevator that will lead you into the store still says, "Dayton's."

But if you push that button today, you'll end up at Macy's.

Chapter 1

The Accidental Merchant

George Draper Dayton never intended to run a department store.
As a boy growing up in New York, he thought he would become a minister. That career aspiration changed in 1873 when a national economic crash interrupted his plan to enroll at Hobart College in Geneva, New York, in September. The Panic of 1873—caused by the country's overinvestment into the railroad business—brought six years of economic depression to the United States and paved the path of Dayton's inadvertent route to the 1902 opening of a store that would become a Minnesota icon for nearly a century.

Bruce B. Dayton tells his grandfather's story in his self-published book, *George Draper Dayton: A Man of Parts*. Concern about the U.S. economy led Dr. David Day Dayton to arrange an apprenticeship for his son rather than send him to college. The sixteen-year-old George Dayton was hired by a local businessman to work in his coal, lumber and nursery businesses. A year later, Dayton was owed more money in commission than the businessman could pay, so he offered to sell Dayton his coal and lumberyard. George Dayton received a quick education in running a business.

Fast-forward eight years: George was now married to Emma Willard Chadwick and the father of David Draper, the first of his four children. Dayton had sold the coal and lumber business and was managing the office of John Mackay, owner of a lumberyard, sawmill and other ventures on Seneca Lake, New York. The national economy was improving, and emigrants from Germany, Scandinavia and Ireland were moving into the country looking for a fresh start. Many of them were headed to Minnesota.

A number of prominent New Yorkers began buying property in Minnesota that year, particularly around the southwestern town of Worthington, where a man named Thomas H. Parsons had bought an interest in the Bank of Worthington and was selling mortgages, bonds and warrants to people in the East. What he didn't tell the buyers was that many of the properties around Worthington had been abandoned.

For years, the area had been hit with one misfortune after another, including the recent national economic slump, unrest between Indians and settlers, grasshopper plagues and severe winter weather. Many farmers were deep in debt, gave up and walked away.

Mortgage-holders in New York found it hard to get answers from Parsons, the "promoter with more imagination than integrity and more mellifluous phrases of encouragement than cash."[1] So twenty-four-year-old George Dayton was sent to appraise the situation firsthand.

He traveled to Minnesota in November 1881. When he returned, he advised investors to place a personal representative in Worthington. A year and a half later, Dayton bought the Bank of Worthington and moved his family—which now included his newborn daughter, Caroline—to the part of the country that was then known as the Northwest.

Dayton ran his first advertisement in the *Worthington Advance* on March 29: "Bank of Worthington. Geo. D. Dayton, Banker and Insurance Agt., Worthington, Nobles County, Minnesota. Does a general banking Business, Buys and sells Exchange. Deals in all kind of Securities. Makes collections. Loans Money on long and short time. Agent for First Class Life and Fire Insurance Cos."[2] Soon, Dayton began acquiring land for the bank and giving loans with easy payments to settlers who were willing to work the land.

By 1884, Dayton had founded the Minnesota Loan and Investment Company, and in 1890 he began looking to make investments outside Worthington and rural Minnesota. Dayton wanted to invest in a city, and after studying property in Chicago, Kansas City, Denver, St. Paul and a few other places, he decided to try Minneapolis. He rented an office downtown and spent time standing on street corners counting passersby. This influenced his decision to buy a piece of land that others thought was too far from the center of town.

In 1892, the *Minneapolis Tribune* reported that property at the corner of Nicollet Avenue and Sixth Street had been sold to George P. Dayton of Worthington (the newspaper printed the wrong middle initial). The paper reported that Dayton had purchased the fifty-five- by ninety-eight-foot property for $2,200 cash—the highest price any Minneapolis real estate had been sold for up to that point.

"G.D. Dayton deals in dry goods / Runs a farm of quite a block, / And—it's libelous to say but— / He believes in watered stock." From *A Port-folio of Cartoons 1915*, published by H.B. Thomson, which featured cartoons and verse about movers and shakers in the Twin Cities in 1915, including businessmen William G. Northrup and Henry Doerr. *Hennepin History Museum.*

Dayton told the newspaper that he intended to construct an eight-story building that he would lease to physicians and surgeons. The building was finished in the fall of 1893, and within weeks, Dayton had purchased another Nicollet Avenue property, this time on Seventh Street and Nicollet, the site of Westminster Presbyterian Church, which had just burned to the ground. Many thought the site, which was adjacent to his first building, was too far out of downtown for a commercial property.

The sale of the property was approved in May 1896. Dayton would not order construction at Seventh and Nicollet for another five years. He still had a bank to run, an investment business and a family back in Worthington.

Folks in Worthington weren't happy about Dayton's purchases in Minneapolis. The *Worthington Globe* reported, "The amount of money

When Emma Dayton moved to Worthington with her children, Draper and Caroline, in May 1883, her family's belongings, including houseplants, were loaded into a rail car in New York and shipped ahead of them. When the car reached Worthington, the plants were frozen.

A number of local women had learned of the frozen plants, and when Emma arrived at her new home in Minnesota, she was greeted with a dining room full of new ones. The kindness the community showed to this woman they had never met was something that George Dayton remembered all of his life.[4]

The Daytons had two more children, Nelson and Josephine. Draper and Caroline finished their school years in Worthington and were off to college when George, Emma, Nelson and Josephine moved to Blaisdell Avenue in Minneapolis in the summer of 1902.

expended on the erection of the Dayton building and the amount needed to improve this property just purchased, if it had been expended here, where it was made, could have greatly enhanced the beauty of our city as well as benefited other property owners. One-third of the purchase price of this property would have put up some excellent business blocks opposite the courthouse where are now some unsightly buildings that detract from the appearance of our business street."[3]

Despite his neighbors' concerns about Dayton's expansion into Minneapolis, he continued to buy property, adding to his Nicollet frontage in 1899 with tracts in the 800 block. In 1900, he purchased fifty feet south of the property he already owned on Seventh Street. By February 1901, he was ready to build.

"Another big business block will grace the northern side of the avenues," the *Minneapolis Tribune* reported. "Geo. D. Dayton, who as the builder of the Dayton and other prominent business blocks on Nicollet Avenue, has repeatedly shown his faith in the future of Minneapolis and in that business street."[5]

The initial plan was to erect a $500,000 hotel at Seventh and Nicollet, but that idea was stalled by a city ordinance. By mid-March, Dayton had published an illustrated plan for that block of Nicollet. Dayton knew he had to secure a major tenant to draw traffic to that part of the city. He persuaded local businessmen J.B. Mosher and George Loudon to buy and move Goodfellow's Dry Goods, the fourth-largest department store in

Goodfellow's opens in the Dayton Building in 1902. *Hennepin County Library.*

the city, from Third Street to the new building. Dayton financed the business and became a silent partner. The twenty-five-year-old store moved into the basement and part of three floors of the building.

On June 24, 1902, Goodfellow's Dry Goods Company opened its Daylight Store to hundreds of shoppers, who, according to one news report, "made purchases, listened to a splendid orchestra and looked with delight at the beautiful goods and beautiful decorations....The new Goodfellow Store—rightly termed the 'Daylight' store—is one of the handsomest and best appointed emporiums in the country."[6]

Chapter 2

Tonight Goodfellow's, Monday Dayton's

G oodfellow's Daylight Store won the praises of the Minneapolis press when it opened at Seventh and Nicollet in June 1902. It was bright and open, and its long, broad "avenues" featured glass showcases with electric lights that illuminated the store's products.

"It is 'new' in every particular and has the very latest and best in everything that goes to make up a great department store," noted the *Minneapolis Journal*. "The first impression one gets of the store is its roominess. There is plenty of 'elbow' and breathing room and the store is immaculate from its splendid basement to its sixth floor."[1]

The store was just one block from the city's leading department store, L.S. Donaldson and Company, which had been at Sixth Street and Nicollet since 1884, and Goodfellow's management knew that it faced stiff competition. So it invested heavily in advertising and strived to offer a variety of merchandise.

By the end of the first year, the store had more than doubled its sales from the previous year at the Third Street location, and George Dayton found himself buying George Loudon's shares in the business after he discovered Loudon's bent toward what he felt were unscrupulous business practices. By the end of the next year, Dayton would also buy out J.B. Mosher.

No longer a silent partner, Dayton took center stage in the business and began making news. On May 2, 1903, Goodfellow's Dry Goods Company offered a stock-purchasing plan to its 240 employees, a practice that was new to this part of the country. The stock plan was good for financial reasons and employee relations.

The George Draper Dayton building in 1902, when Goodfellow's Dry Goods opened for business. *Hennepin County Library.*

Dayton told the *Journal* that he believed in "the cultivation of the most kindly feeling between the firm and its employees. If we give the employees this opportunity it will cement the pleasant relations."[2]

Two weeks later, on May 18, the store ran an ad in the *Journal* announcing a Reorganization Sale that would mark a name change to the business. Five days later, another *Journal* ad announced "Tonight Goodfellow's—Monday (The Daylight Store) Dayton's." George's oldest son, D. Draper Dayton, a recent Princeton graduate who had taken a job in the store as a "bundle boy" in the first year, was listed as an officer of the store in the advertisement.

Above: Dayton's Dry Goods Company. *Hennepin County Library.*

Left: Seventh Street, looking west from Marquette Avenue, downtown Minneapolis, in about 1910. You can see the Dayton's sign in the upper-middle part of the photo. *Hennepin County Library.*

Under its new name, Dayton's Dry Goods Company, the store extended its stock program to the public. In an effort to raise more capital to expand the store, Dayton's offered residents of Minnesota, North Dakota, South Dakota and Wisconsin $200,000 of its 6 percent preferred stock.

Newspaper notices invited men to purchase stock in their wives' or daughters' names: "The ladies will find a pleasure in thus investing some of their surplus funds and owning a part of the store where they can so conveniently trade, and where they can so pleasantly introduce their friends."[3]

The stock program generated plenty of free publicity and support for the new company. Two years after the first offering, the *Evening Tribune* reported that Dayton's stock plan did just what Dayton had hoped it would do: "Hundreds of representative people purchased shares in the new company, and everyone who purchased a share became practically a partner."[4]

Customer loyalty was key to the store's success, and Dayton's continued to generate it through a variety of promotions. A three-day Inventory Sale in June offered bargains for shoppers at all income levels. Free concerts and free lunches were advertised. The store motto, "What's

An undated photo of employees in the Dayton's Drapery Department. *Hennepin History Museum.*

Wrong We'll Right," encouraged shoppers to alert management to any misleading advertisements. Customers received one dollar for each wrong they brought to the store's attention.

Dayton's also continued to give incentives to its employees, which built employee allegiance to the company and generated the goodwill of organized labor. The store gave workers a half day off on Fridays in July and August and began offering a full week of vacation with full pay to employees who had served one continuous year. Labor newspapers described the company's officers as "broad-minded" and "public-spirited."

Hundreds of shares were sold in the spring of 1903, and the store grew, adding several leased departments that year, including Merkham Trading Company's "hair-curler" parlor, Emma Read's drawing supplies, Mrs. Gertrude Stanton's optical service and, in the basement of the building, W.B. Sayre's hardware, china and glassware. The store also offered a desk where customers could check their parcels and have them delivered to the train station in time for their departure home.

In 1905, the store leased space for a furniture department and the next year added a bookstore. The fourth floor saw the opening of a piano department and a salon leased by a local dressmaker, "Miss Helen."

Minneapolis streetscape, circa 1904–8. *Hennepin County Library.*

Draper was named general manager in 1906. George kept his office and a presence at the store. He also continued to work in the real estate and financial aspects of the company.

In August 1906, Dayton's opened what the *Daily News* described as "new and spacious tearooms": a colonial room with columns marking the separation of the room's six "sextagonal" booths; a Gothic room with tall brown columns and arches that "give the effect of a cathedral nave" and served as the store's smoking room, "the especial realm of the men, who may here enjoy not only a delightful repast, but the after-dinner cigar as well"; and a banquet hall where clubs and fraternities were invited to hold their annual affairs "and club women may congregate for luncheon."[5]

Five years after the store's opening, George Dayton's time spent in the late 1800s counting passersby on a Minneapolis corner paid off. The *Minneapolis Journal* noted that the store had "brought the shopping public up the avenue and paved the way for other shops until now Dayton's store can be said to be in the very heart of the shopping district."[6] Dayton's benefited even more when the elegant Radisson Hotel—named after French explorer Pierre Radisson—opened next door in 1909.

As the store's first decade rolled on, management continued to add benefits for Dayton's employees.

STORE DON'TS

The Dayton Dry Goods Company printed a handbook in 1905 listing sixty-four "don'ts" for employees. Here are just a few of them.

DON'T wait upon customers with your hands dirty or your fingernails in mourning.

DON'T chase customers! Wait till they stop and show that they are interested in goods or some department, then approach them in a business-like manner.

DON'T greet your customer with a beer, tobacco or onion breath. It hastens them to move on to more fragrant surroundings.

DON'T be discourteous to customers. It's a fault which cannot be excused.

DON'T misrepresent goods. You can sell more without. "A pleased customer, always a customer."

DON'T disparage other stores or people connected with same. Keep silent rather than make any uncomplimentary remarks of business neighbors.

DON'T accept a position unless you are perfectly willing and anxious to follow the rules of the store in every detail pleasantly and efficiently.[7]

In the summer of 1908, Dayton's announced that it would close early on Saturday evenings throughout the months of July and August, except on the last Saturday in August, when the Minnesota State Fair would fill the cities of Minneapolis and St. Paul with visitors from all over the state.

Dayton's summer gift to employees was quickly one-upped by a competitor, the Minneapolis Dry Goods Company, which announced in the *Minneapolis Journal* that it would close both Saturday afternoons and evenings in the summer.

In March 1909, Dayton's added a new basement store that would cater to customers "who wish to buy dependable…and creditable merchandise but can't afford, or don't want to pay more than is absolutely necessary to secure these qualities," George Dayton told the *Minneapolis Journal*.[8] The "Bargain Basement" offered lower prices than the upper floors and stocked women's coats, suits and dresses, along with linens, corsets, millinery, jewelry, underwear, notions and laces. It also included the china department, a music department, a thirty-two-foot soda fountain and a candy department.

Toward the end of that year, George Dayton staged his first novel publicity stunt. In November, Dayton's third floor hosted Glenn Curtiss's biplane, which had recently won a race in France. Minneapolis was the fourth city to host the Curtiss Airship exhibit, and it generated the positive public relations Dayton was looking for. The *Minneapolis Journal* ran two photos on the front page.

In 1911, the corporation changed its name to the Dayton Company. The first nine-story section of the building was completed in the rear of the original structure on Seventh Street that year, and the third floor opened in time to celebrate the store's ninth anniversary on Nicollet and Seventh.

The *Tribune* described the floors as a "dream place for women": "Nothing could be more elegant or diffuse an air of such utter luxury. Of mahogany woodwork of artistic and costly design there is no end, and treading the green velvet carpet is like strolling the golf links. Here are the millinery and the suits, party dresses, skirts, and the ensemble looks like the scene of a garden party. There are private dressing and fitting rooms, and dainty little inclosures [sic] where milady may have the new Easter hats poised upon her pretty head beyond the purview of the throng."[9]

Chapter 3

Nelson Joins the Dayton Company

The name change from Dayton Dry Goods Company to the Dayton Company was not the only significant event for the store in 1911: Nelson Dayton joined his brother and father in the business that year.

Like his father, Nelson hadn't intended to be a merchant. He wanted to be a farmer. His childhood spent in rural Worthington fostered a love of farm animals and agriculture, and after spending two years at Macalester College (the Presbyterian college in St. Paul that George Dayton supported), Nelson decided to pursue a career in farming. He enrolled in the School of Agriculture at the University of Minnesota and earned a bachelor's degree in 1907. Shortly after graduation, Nelson's father helped him buy Oak Leaf Farm, a 4,800-acre spread in Anoka County. For the next four years, Nelson struggled to make the farm successful.

By 1911, he had a change of heart and gave in to the coaxing from his father and brother. He joined the Dayton Company as a blanket buyer, an area in which the store did not hold a lead in the region. For several seasons, Nelson bought the best blankets available and sold them at cost, which helped build customer loyalty and the prestige of the department.

Draper and Nelson were now equal partners in the business, as they each owned one-third of the store. Their father gave one-twelfth to each of their two sisters, Caroline and Josephine. George; his wife, Emma; and the Dayton Investment Company held the rest of the common stock.

The Dayton brothers led the store through continuing expansion. In 1913, an annex that included a subbasement, basement and one-story shops was

George Nelson Dayton, many years after he joined the company. *Hennepin County Library.*

completed at the corner of Eighth and Nicollet, giving the store its first Eighth Street entrance. That year, Dun and Company (later Dun and Bradstreet, a financial information provider) listed the company's net worth at more than $1 million. In 1914, eight floors were added to the annex built the previous year.

George spent less time on store affairs, although he still kept his hand in the business, and as president, George was the company spokesperson. When Germany declared war in Europe in 1914, Dayton's ran three large ads signed, "George D. Dayton," declaring the Dayton Company's confidence in the region's economic future and promised to "take care of our customers." One ad countered a report that implied the

The February 1917 fire shut down Dayton's for ten days. *Hennepin History Museum.*

war would hinder silk and dye goods from being brought into the Northwest and promised a grand annual silk sale at the store.

The Daytons seemed fixed on proving that Minneapolis's economy was sound, and in 1916, the store broadened its frontage on Eighth Street to 150 feet. "We have again outgrown our building," George Dayton told the *Minneapolis Tribune*. "The store is many times as large as when it came to its present location in 1902, which then was considered somewhat 'uptown,' but which now is the heart of the retail district." Dayton's now ran around three sides of the block between Seventh and Eighth Streets in buildings ranging from two to nine stories.[1]

Just months later, in the early morning hours of February 17, 1917, a night watchman discovered flames in the two-story Dayton building at the corner of Eighth Street and Nicollet Avenue. The fire was thought to have started in the shoe shop, and high winds quickly fanned the flames, according to a news article in the February 18, 1917 edition of the *Minneapolis Tribune*.

Firefighters fought through the night in subzero weather and were able to confine the fire to

THE CUSTOMER IS ALWAYS RIGHT, EVEN WHEN SHE'S NOT

Dayton's was known for its liberal customer-service policies. Starting with its "What's Wrong We'll Right" policy established at its onset, the store managed to please its customers by sticking to a generous return policy.

In 1913, master rug salesman John Karagheusian managed to convince a woman to purchase the Oriental rug she was admiring. He promised her that the colors in the rug would intensify with age, that the rug's value would increase and that if in fifteen years she no longer wanted the rug, she could bring it back to the Dayton Company and Karagheusian himself would buy it back at the purchase price.

She bought the rug, and a decade and a half later, she carried it back into the store. She wanted her money back. Tastes in home décor had changed. Karagheusian hadn't anticipated that Oriental rugs would no longer be in demand fifteen years after the sale. Despite the salesman's protests, management decided that a bargain's a bargain. The woman was refunded the full purchase price of the rug.

Management's philosophy was that buying the goodwill of a customer through the price of a returned garment was a good deal for the store.[2] "It isn't a question of whether the customer is right or wrong," Nelson Dayton was quoted, "it is a question merely of whether she thinks she is right."

the building that housed the shoe and silk departments, the storage basement and a second floor with a restaurant and schoolrooms for employees. Those were the only areas of the store not protected by automatic sprinklers. The store's new buildings and the original Dayton Building were not involved in the fire, thanks to heavy fire walls and steel doors that shut those areas away from the small shops in what was then called the Narragansett Block.

Loss at the Dayton's store was estimated at between $250,000 and $500,000. Much of the damage to the buildings was from water and smoke. George D. Dayton announced immediately after the fire that the store would be ready to open the following Wednesday, but two days later, he announced that the extent of the damage and the absence of thirty department managers who were out of town created unexpected delays.

"We do not know just yet what the total damage will amount to," Dayton told the *Minneapolis Tribune*. "Besides the burning of the shoe department, water and smoke damaged practically every department. The last of the water was pumped out of the basement yesterday and by noon we had fires under the boilers. …We have restored heat in the store, and hope to be able to resume business soon."[3]

The store reopened after ten days, and customers were greeted with a big sale of items that were exposed to smoke or fire. Thousands of shoppers showed up that first day. At times, the store had to close the doors to control the crowds. The store ran an ad in the next day's paper apologizing to its customers, explaining that it needed to do that to take care of the customers who were already inside the building. Because sales of the smoke-damaged goods went so well, the store added more inventory to the sale with goods that had already been in stock but weren't exposed to the smoke or water.

The fire hastened the company's plans to build a new structure at the corner of Nicollet and Eighth: a three-story fireproof building to replace the building that burned. The new building would serve as the first unit of a planned twelve stories. "We have had plans for a corner building for some time," George Dayton told the *Minneapolis Tribune*, "and those are being looked into as a result of the fire which suddenly has disorganized our operating system."[4]

One other phoenix that rose from that fire was the transformation of the Bargain Basement. Draper Dayton saw the damage from the fire as a chance to begin again in the discount store. He handed the management of the lower-level store to C.J. Larson, who renamed it the Downstairs Store. Larson made sure that the new store was brightly lit. Nine elevators and ten stairways led customers to the lower level.

A refurbished Dayton's in 1917, after the fire. *Hennepin County Library.*

A Dayton's delivery wagon in 1918. *Hennepin History Museum.*

A MAN'S PERSONALITY IS
REFLECTED IN HIS BUSINESS
From Women's Wear, *July 1914*

Every great establishment reflects in some degree, throughout its length and breadth, the personality of the man at its head. All over the Dayton store in Minneapolis is the stamp of George D. Dayton....[H]e takes, out of the profits of his business, goodly sum for the betterment of his own working people. His rest rooms and clubrooms, his school of instruction for girls who have not had opportunity for education, his profit-sharing plan at holiday time and other like efforts have done much good. He is proud of the high character of his employees, and always thinking up some plan for their benefit.[6]

The basement wasn't used as a dumping ground for goods that couldn't be sold elsewhere. It sold "popularly priced" goods that people wanted. Each section of the store had its own buyer. In 1917, a shopper could find a pair of slippers for $0.69, a shotgun for $350.00 and a fur coat $400.00.[5]

The spring of 1917 brought more change to the store as Dayton's employees began to leave to fight in World War I. Eighty-four men left the Dayton's ranks, but they were promised their jobs when they returned.

Also that year, twenty-eight employees were members of the first graduating class of the school established by George Dayton just a few years before for employees who had not finished high school. George wanted his workers to become "large-minded, intelligent men and women who would grow into better positions and thus become more valuable to themselves, to their employers, and to the world." Draper's sister-in-law, Ima Winchell Stacy, developed the curriculum, which included mastery of spelling, penmanship, arithmetic, composition, salesmanship and knowledge of textiles. She also helped organize a Shakespeare group, a travel group and a music class and led a team of women that made 24,431 surgical dressings for the Red Cross that were sent to the military units fighting overseas in the spring of 1918.[7]

The staff's morale and well-being were important to George Dayton, and the school for workers was just one of a number of initiatives that helped the store create a community that both management and employees began calling "Daytonia."

Chapter 4

High Morale and High Flight

The high morale of store employees was a priority for the company patriarch, and the familial warmth that George Dayton wished to extend to his workers was expressed every Christmas Eve at closing time. Store managers lined up at the door to greet employees and wish them a happy holiday as they left the building, and George was there handing a box of candy to each of them.

The company hosted employee parties and dinners, and workers joined baseball teams, bowling teams, glee clubs, orchestras and other activities that fostered a community life there. George often called impromptu store meetings in the tearoom with the entire staff, or he'd speak from the balcony above the main floor to the employees below and discuss public affairs and how events in the greater world might affect the store. He sent personal notes to employees before a sale encouraging them to make it the best sale ever, and he sent thank-you notes after the sales, commending employees for their work.

When 1,500 employees were left without work during the ten days after the 1917 fire, they were paid for those missed days. The men who enlisted or were drafted during World War I were offered their jobs back when they returned. (Many of them did return, and some stayed to become executives at the company.)

In the 1962 book *You Can Get It at Dayton's*, James Gray described the results of George Dayton's efforts at "communicating a warm sense of hospitality" to his employees: "There was but little doubt that the loyalty of its staff made a significant contribution to the early success of the store or that this

WBAH

In the spring of 1922, Nelson Dayton launched one more first at the store: a radio station. WBAH Radio was one of only six radio stations in Minneapolis and the first radio broadcast station to be operated by a department store in the Twin Cities. It was also the first in the area to use a battery rather than a generator to power the station.

On May 11, 1922, advertising manager Hugh Arthur formally opened WBAH with an announcement "of its call and its aim." Arthur's words were followed by a brief piano solo by store employee Dayne Donovan.

The station had its fits and starts and operated for only two years. Listeners liked the free entertainment, and Dayton executives liked the free advertising, but they wanted the station to reach farther than it did. WBAH was rebuilt to enhance its reception in 1923 and was heard as far as California when it reopened in October. Eventually, its broadcasts could be heard in Europe.

The *Minneapolis Tribune* ran a story on April 27, 1924, that reported that the station had received a letter from Berlin; the letter writer had "heard the concert of Macalester College and the Third Infantry band, which were broadcast by the station."

Despite its increased range, just two months after WBAH observed its second birthday with music by Tenie Murphy Sheehan, soprano, and Lucille Frankman Murphy, accompanist, the store got out of the radio business. The station equipment was given as a Christmas present to the Dunwoody Institute in Minneapolis.

Apparently, Willy BAH, as the station had come to be known, lived on for a time after it shut down. On November 2, 1924, the *Minneapolis Journal* reported that "Willy BAH's Ghost Howls in 2 Nations": "Somewhere up in the empty, eerie ether, the ghost of Willy Bah howled and sputtered and sang last night." The paper went on to report that Dayton's had received a number of letters from people who said they had heard broadcasts coming from WBAH, even though the station had been dead for exactly three months and three days.

The same thing had happened with the *Journal*'s defunct station, WBAD, which had shut down its broadcasts two years before: "In both cases, listeners apparently had heard some other station, missed the call letters, consulted a call book—and decided it was a Minneapolis station," the paper noted.

loyalty sprang spontaneously out of the family atmosphere that enclosed the daily routine."

The store had a profit-sharing incentive at Christmas that gave salespeople 2 percent of their sales (up to thirty-five dollars) made during the fifteen days before Christmas. Other workers would receive a gift of five or ten dollars each, depending on their length of service.

In July 1918, the store began publishing the *Daytonews*, an employee bulletin that reported news from each department, listed employee birthdays for the month, announced engagements and weddings and published wise words from George. The publication aspired to be "a chronicle of store events and a cheer sheet for every one who reads it." In the November issue that year, just before the World War I armistice was announced on November 11, the store promised an employee fair: a "mad bedlam of fun—a gloom chaser deluxe." The fair was intended to introduce employees to all the new merchandise coming in for the Christmas season, and it became an annual event.

Dayton's established a Welfare Department in 1919. It was created and managed by Jane Sargent, who had been head of the store's mail-order department. Sargent was charged with helping employees who needed to obtain credit or help paying their bills or buying a house, or even solving a problem with a boss.

James Gray described "Daytonia" as the spirit that made the store an institution, and it spread beyond the store. In 1916, the Dayton Company created a new position tasked with spreading the store's energy and creativity to consumers: advertising manager. Hugh Arthur, a former newspaper editor and advertising director, became Dayton's P.T. Barnum. Dedicating 4 percent of the advertising budget to publicity stunts, he used "the latest facilities of transportation and communication to give the life of the store the air of being a day or two ahead of tomorrow. Customers loved the stunts, watched for more, speculated about what the next would be—and talked about Dayton's."[1]

When Dayton's made news in September 1919 for hiring planes to deliver the goods that out-of-town visitors ordered at the Minnesota State Fair, it generated good public relations but also piqued the public's interest in commercial flight. Dayton's merchandise was flown to eighteen destinations northwest of Minneapolis that fall, including to a wedding, where a gift was delivered just before the ceremony began.

The next spring, George Dayton took advantage of an express handlers' rail strike in New York to experiment with moving merchandise via air. Working with his neighbor William Kidder, owner of Curtiss Northwest

Curtiss Northwest airplanes were used for many Dayton's promotions. Here, Ray Miller, one of the pilots hired in 1920 to deliver goods from New York to Minneapolis, is seated in a plane at Curtiss Northwest Airport. *Minnesota Aviation Hall of Fame.*

A Curtiss Jenny plane at Curtiss Northwest Airport with a Dayton's label. *Minnesota Aviation Hall of Fame.*

Airplane Company, headquartered right by the fairgrounds, Dayton hired two planes (painted with the words "Dayton's Delivery") to fly from New York to Minneapolis with eight hundred pounds of merchandise.

The two pilots, Ray Miller and Charles Keys, were already heading to New York to fly two de Havilland planes to Montana. They loaded the planes with the Dayton Company goods, with plans to stop in Minneapolis en route. The flyers battled rain and high winds and made numerous stops before landing the planes at the parade grounds across from Dunwoody Institute in Minneapolis on May 10, 1920. The planes' wings were removed, and the pilots promptly drove the fuselages through downtown streets and made a street-side delivery to Dayton's.

The merchandise (jewelry, lace, men's silk shirts and other sundries) was immediately brought into the store, and every item—bearing tags that read, "By Airplane from New York to Minneapolis for the Dayton Co"—was purchased by shoppers looking for souvenirs from this historic flight.

The shipment wasn't a moneymaker for Dayton's. It cost $2,500 to ship $6,000 worth of merchandise, but at the time, the two-thousand-plus-mile flight was the longest commercial flight on record, and the publicity was priceless. Before the flights actually happened, New York City newspapers sent out dispatches about the imminent journey.

The event led to other attention-seeking flights for the company. As for William Kidder, he went on to form a company that took over the airmail contract between Chicago and the Twin Cities. The company's name was Northwest Airways, which eventually became Northwest Orient Airlines (and Minnesota readers know the rest of that story).

The next year, Dayton's sent out planes to fly over the grounds of eighty-eight county fairs and the annual Paul Bunyan celebration in Brainerd, dropping foot-long red, blue and yellow feathers that bore the Dayton name.

AVIATION HAZARDS

The Dayton Company's early days experimenting with commercial flight coincided with the early days of prohibition. George D. Dayton was a teetotaler and known for his religious views and strong moral principles. Roger Bergerson, author of *Winging It at a Country Crossroads*, tells this story in his book:

Dayton brought a photographer out to Curtiss Northwest airport one day to take some pictures of a plane with "Dayton's" painted on it. After a bit, one such plane returned from North Dakota and [William] Kidder introduced Dayton to the pilot, noticing that the front cockpit was covered with canvas.

Disingenuous as it now seems, as Kidder later told the story, he was horrified to learn that the cargo was a load of Canadian whiskey. He allegedly told the pilot, "If old Mr. Dayton had seen that whiskey in there, he'd have had you and me both in jail!"

Unfazed, the pilot responded, "Well, you know Mr. Kidder, that's one of the hazards of aviation!"

The year 1922 marked Dayton's twentieth anniversary. The *Minneapolis Sunday Tribune* reported that the anniversary demonstrated "George D. Dayton's confidence in Minneapolis as a growing community and his courage in locating his store at a point where, a score of years ago, big retail stores were not located. Today the Dayton store stands in the center of the city's retail shopping district."[2]

The store celebrated with a large ad praising both the customers of the store and its employees and by holding its annual anniversary sale. Later that year, Dayton's announced a one-day Golden Jubilee Bargain Day on October 11. Double quantities of goods were ordered, prices were slashed and the sale was promoted heavily. "We are determined to do the largest day's business ever done by any store in the Northwest," read an ad. The sale was such a success that for the first time the store pushed Donaldson's out of the no. 1 retail spot in the region, and the annual Jubilee Sale was established.

Dayton's was at the top of its game. In 1923, Draper and Nelson bought their sisters' shares of the store. Nelson retired the debt he had with his Anoka farm, his share of the store and a house and lot on Blaisdell Avenue, and George began turning more attention to philanthropy and real estate.

Then something happened that changed the course at the Dayton Company: Draper Dayton died of heart failure at the age of forty-three.

Chapter 5

A Decade of Flux

D raper Dayton was forty-three when he died at his summer home in
Minnetonka on July 25, 1923, just two days after he had fallen ill while
playing an after-work golf game. He had been seeing a doctor for some
health issues in recent weeks, but his sudden illness that Monday night in
July was thought to be a severe case of indigestion. Cause of death was
determined to be heart failure.

Front-page headlines announced Draper's death in the local papers:
"D. Draper Dayton Dies Suddenly at Minnetonka Home" and
"Merchant Succumbs After 2 Day Illness." The Dayton Company ran
an ad announcing that the store would be closed all day on July 27 so
that employees could attend Draper's funeral, and many of the store's
competitors ran mourning ads, including L.S. Donaldson Company,
Powers and E.E. Athkinson and Company.

The week after the funeral, George Dayton spoke to employees from the
stairs leading to the balcony of the store. He announced that he would take
back more responsibility in the store and that Nelson would assume many
of Draper's duties. "But we cannot do it all," he said, "for I have sometimes
said Draper was equal to five men. You will help, we know, and seek in many
ways to make good the loss of Draper."[1]

The store had already been dealing with the death of two important store
managers that year: Ray Arnold, the store's controller, and Franklin Spear,
the third-floor merchandising manager. Then, just two weeks after Draper's
death, George spoke at another funeral: that of Ima Winchell Stacy, the
woman who created Dayton's employee-education program.

Nelson bought Draper's share of the common stock and began building a new executive team. C.J. Larson, who had been in charge of the Downstairs Store, was named general merchandise manager. John Per-Lee was named assistant general manager, Hugh Arthur was named publicity director and John Luker was named vice-president and divisional merchandise manager. Nelson also brought in personnel director W.E. Parmeter and merchandise manager David Birkett. The new team joined controller W.A. Dillman, who was hired to replace Ray Arnold in January 1923, as well as store superintendent A.C. White and divisional merchandise manager Alan Phillips.

Nelson began refining the store's philosophy of service to the public, emphasizing these three points:

- Capture the customers' imaginations with an array of goods.
- Earn loyalty with a generous merchandising policy.
- Provide incidental attractions and conveniences within Dayton's walls so customers do not wander to the doors of competitors.[2]

Attractions and conveniences were certainly something that the Twin Cities community came to expect from the store in the coming decades.

Management did not rest and continued to plan improvements and increases in the store's size. "If we are to build in 1928, as I believe we should, there is not time to lose," wrote George to Nelson in a letter in early 1926. "I favor large provision for tearooms, kitchen, foyer, rest rooms, etc. I favor an auditorium and large office facilities. I favor escalators at least to the third floor, possibly higher."

The cover of *Daytonews*, January 1926. *Hennepin County Library.*

Vol. XI   JANUARY 1926   No. 1

A little magazine published once a month by the employees of The Dayton Company, Minneapolis, Minnesota. It aspires to be a chronicle of store events and a cheer sheet for every one who reads it.

The price of THE DAYTONEWS is 3c per copy. On the day of publication it will be on sale at the 7th St. entrance, the 8th St. entrance, and the 10th floor cafeteria.

Happy New Year to You

How easy it is to say it! And we really mean it when we say it.

But did you ever stop to think that after all it is the other person who must put forth the effort necessary to vitalize the wish? Our "Happy New Year to you" is the expression of our kindly desire—it is the outcropping of our benevolence of thought—and we really, truly wish we could make the New Year very HAPPY indeed to all those we so freely "wish" it for. The "wish" often benefits us more than those to whom we say it— for our expression cheers, sweetens, broadens, ennobles us, and our lives are happier because we "wish" happiness for those about us.

But we all must bestir ourselves in order to achieve real happiness—it cannot come to any simply by our "wish," no matter how sincere that "wish" may have been. And haven't we all found by experience that the surest, and really the only way, to become happy is to forget ourselves in efforts to serve, cheer, encourage others?

Retroaction is a large word, but it covers a world of thought and philosophy —whenever we honestly seek to help any one we actually are more helped than is he, for it all reacts on us. I cannot explain it, but it is true that our simple wishing every one we meet a "Happy New Year" so reacts on us that before we know it we find ourselves "walking on air" and become conscious we are happy through and through because we have wished happiness to others. Let's fill the air the next few days with our wishes that all around us may have a really, truly very "Happy New Year."

With all my heart I wish it for every one connected with the Dayton organization. If I could, I would shield you all from anything that would make it less than a very "Happy New Year."

Geo. D. Dayton

A message from George Dayton to his employees, January 1926. *Hennepin County Library.*

KEEPING THE SABBATH

George D. Dayton was a deeply religious man and carried his Presbyterian-based principles into the company: No liquor was sold, the store would not advertise in a newspaper that sponsored liquor ads, the store was closed on Sunday and Dayton's would never advertise on a Sunday. Even when asked by customers to keep the Christmas display windows lit on Sundays, George declined.

Nelson, whose five sons were all working in the store by the 1940s and would take over the business in 1950, recognized that times were changing and told his sons that the store would not advertise on Sunday in his lifetime, but he would remove the prohibition from the bylaws so that the "five boys" would be free to do so when they deemed it necessary.[3] George Dayton's Sunday rules would see their end in the 1960s.

Cars jam the streets to see holiday decorations at Dayton's in 1939. During George Dayton's time at the store, lights were out on Sundays, even during Christmas. *Hennepin History Museum.*

The aim: "Put the store so far ahead of anything in [the] Twin Cities that everyone will be filled with amazement."[4] And that's what they did.

The store's silver anniversary in 1927 aimed to amaze and attract consumers. Before its Silver Anniversary Sale in February 1927, Dayton's went on a hunt for coins minted in 1902, offering to pay $0.15 apiece for dimes, $0.35 for quarters, $0.65 for half dollars and $1.25 for dollars. In all, 43,022 pieces were bought and placed in a store window at the corner of Seventh Street and Nicollet Avenue. They were displayed for fifty-two hours and had a guard posted around the clock both inside and outside for the whole showing.

A collection of rare silver pieces was displayed first in the Nicollet Avenue windows and then in the store. The exhibit contained more than $125,000 worth of silver that included a candelabra made for Britain's Queen Anne and a snuffbox once presented by a Dutch queen to the sultan of Sarawak. Many of the pieces were selected from museums around the world, including New York's Metropolitan Museum of Art and the British Museum.

KEYS TO SUCCESS

In December 1927, George D. Dayton gave a talk to an evening class of more than one hundred students at the Minneapolis YMCA and listed the qualities he said were essential to success: honesty, truthfulness, initiative, courage, enthusiasm, self-respect and courtesy.

George D. Dayton. *Hennepin County Library.*

The store produced six exclusive WCCO radio broadcasts of Minneapolis Symphony Orchestra concerts, which kicked off in November. The concerts were the symphony's first radio broadcasts and coincided with the silver anniversaries of both the orchestra and the Dayton Company.

Dayton's silver anniversary year also brought its first store branch, which was set up near the University of Minnesota campus in Minneapolis. The three-story University Store featured women's wear on the first floor, men's on the second and a tearoom called the Tent on the third floor. Hung with draperies to give it the exotic atmosphere of a sheik's tent, it was popular among the college crowd and ran out of food quickly each day.

Soon, a second restaurant, the Dungeon, was opened in the basement. The Dungeon featured waiters who dressed in prison stripes. Its walls were decorated with balls and chains.

In 1928, the Dayton Company added a four-story parking garage on Eighth Street that could house three hundred automobiles. That same year, the store received the first merchandise to reach America from Europe by air. On October 16, 1928, the store ran an advertisement in the *Minneapolis Journal* announcing that the company had received a wire that morning heralding a shipment "of some of the first merchandise ever to reach America by air... just removed from dirigible Graf Zeppelin STOP sending to you air mail...R M C Day." (Day was the manager of Dayton's Berlin office.)

In the summer of 1929, the Dayton Company purchased J.B. Hudson and Son, a forty-five-year-old jewelry store. In October, the seemingly robust national economy came to a sudden halt. The stock market crashed.

Chapter 6

Selling through the Great Depression

The decade following the 1929 stock market crash began with both financial and personal loss for the Dayton family. Although the store managed to stay profitable through the Depression years following the crash, the economic collapse was difficult for George and Emma Dayton. They had put most of their fortune into the Dayton Foundation, and their property values had plummeted, but George, who still held the title of president of the Dayton Company, collected a salary from the store. Nelson kept his father on the payroll, paying him the same salary he paid himself, until George died in 1938.

Emma died in 1931. George stayed involved in the company after his beloved wife's death, but he could not bring himself to attend the store's Christmas party that year without her.

Nationally, December 1931 brought little cheer: the year ended with New York's Bank of the United States (with more than $200 million in deposits) collapsing, making it the largest single bank failure in the nation's history.

George Dayton had been optimistic that the Northwest would weather the Depression better than other areas of the country because of its dependence on agriculture rather than manufacturing. In many parts of the state, that was true. Yet in April 1932, he spoke to employees at a storewide dinner about how the economy had brought the entire nation "down from the false pinnacle of prosperity built on a foundation of sand. How long the present depression will last no one can tell."[1]

The winners in the Dayton Company's "No Accident Drivers" competition in 1930–31, with George Dayton (far left). *Hennepin History Museum.*

In Hennepin County, more than sixty-eight thousand people were unemployed in the winter of 1932–33. Unemployment climbed to almost 30 percent in Minneapolis in 1933.[2]

The Dayton Company kept up an energetic fight by continuing to buy products in large quantities and then sell them at the lowest possible price. The Downstairs Store instituted Early Bird sales on Saturdays from 9:00 a.m. to noon. One of the lower-level store's main attractions was the daily bargain in the Red Arrow Booth, which customers could find by following the huge symbols painted on the floor pointing the way.

The store tried to pay for merchandise before it was received to save the money it would pay in interest. Those savings were passed on to the shopper. Management began focusing on specific departments to increase sales volume. In one example, a buyer filled a train car with 1,164 overcoats from a mill in Gallison, Ohio, much to the delight of the small manufacturing town. When the coats arrived in Minneapolis, Dayton's advertised the coat sale and displayed nothing but those coats in its show windows and down the middle aisle of the store.

The first day, enough items were sold to make the sale one of the store's most successful.

HE COULD LEAD THE MASSES ON TO BATTLE AND VICTORY

Jeanne Auerbacher joined Dayton's in the 1930s and rose to buyer of the Oval Room through the 1940s and 1950s. These notes are from an undated talk she gave at the store and are printed with permission from the Goldstein Museum of Design at the University of Minnesota.

One could have heard a pin drop to the floor. I did not know what it all meant, when I suddenly saw a wheelchair being brought in. In it sat a gentleman, a most unusual gentleman. Nobody had to tell me who he was. This beautiful strong head, those finely chiseled features, those eyes, stern and kindly both, commanding and still showing a little twinkle that only people have who truly know and truly understand, it could only be Mr. Dayton, the founder of this very store.

He spoke a few words, simple words, but words that pulled the heartstrings of everyone listening. Many an old-timer's eyes became moist, many a throat felt choked, and never have I seen such reverence and admiration written in everyone's face, as these people showed for this great old gentleman. His must have been the power and magic of heroes of the days past, whose command could lead the masses on to battle and victory.

The orchestra played a song, his song, a simple tune of the *yeller* ribbon and the sweetheart *fur fur* away. And I sang it along with these hundreds of admiring, happy people. Suddenly I was not a stranger anymore. I entered a silent partnership with this man and felt proud to belong to a place that was built on integrity and fine leadership.

The store used a cornucopia symbol overflowing with trains and trucks loaded with goods in its print advertisements during this time. That horn of plenty epitomized the store's abundance of merchandise.

In the November 1932 election, Americans cast 22.8 million votes for Franklin D. Roosevelt and his platform, which called for unemployment assistance, old-age insurance, labor laws, farmers' assistance, a repeal of prohibition and more. Roosevelt won, and although George Dayton was a Herbert Hoover man, he told employees at a post-election store meeting that

INVISIBLE GLASS WINDOW
AT DAYTON COMPANY
MYSTIFIES THRONGS

"Window shoppers and pavement gawkers were lined up three deep in front of a certain window on Nicollet Avenue today," reported the *Minneapolis Journal* on September 24, 1936. The occasion was the first invisible glass window in that part of the country. The window appeared to have no glass protecting the merchandise from the viewers.

"Mainstay in the illusion is a large sheet of bent glass, 8 feet, 5 inches wide by 11 feet, 6 inches high, which sweeps back from the store front for 4 feet, 8 inches," the *Journal* reported. "On the sides there are four mirrors. Across the top is a strip of black velvet and the entire background is hung with a black drape."

The result was an open-looking show window without the glare and reflections of an ordinary window. Spectators looked at the display behind the window and felt that they could reach out and touch the merchandise. The innovative window was one of only eleven installations throughout the country. The others were in New York, Chicago and San Francisco.

they were fortunate to have "a form of government that makes possible a revolution by using ballots instead of bullets."[3]

Roosevelt's inauguration in March 1933 coincided with the new president's bank holiday, which suspended banking transactions from a Monday to Thursday, while Congress worked to pass the Emergency Banking Act designed to reopen banks that were solvent and assist those that were not. The Monday the banks closed, Dayton's officers called Minneapolis churches and offered to take any unbanked cash from the Sunday collection plates and give checks in exchange, essentially turning the store into a bank itself. Checks of reasonable size were cashed for customers in good standing. Employees whose salaries were in the middle to low bracket received cash in their weekly pay envelopes rather than a check.

In June, the National Recovery Administration (NRA) was established to aid businesses by creating codes of "fair competition" and to set prices, minimum wages and maximum work hours. Although the Supreme Court eventually ruled that the NRA infringed on the separation of powers under the U.S. Constitution, it instigated some labor practices that were popular with workers. Firms were asked to display the Blue Eagle, an emblem that signified that the company was participating in the NRA program. Businesses that didn't display that eagle were often boycotted.

Whether or not Dayton's managers were NRA supporters, in November 1933, the store ran an ad in the *Minneapolis Journal* that featured a drawing of Santa Claus holding a National Recovery Administration button with the eagle and exclaiming, "I'll Do My Part!" The ad was aimed at getting the economy back on firmer footing by encouraging the public to spend: "I'll do my part! I'll put men to work; I'll put women in the happy flurry and bustle of roasting and baking; and I'll stuff a popcorn ball into the eager mouth of a child. I'll even make *you* happier and wealthier. Will you help me?"

Santa implored readers to remember "all those who have been on your Christmas list in generous years past": "GIVING creates employment— employment creates giving, over and over again. Back and forth it echoes until the air is charged with Christmas cheer. And very soon this servant you have sent out on a mission to create wealth and gladness will return to you with larger gifts of material benefit, to say: 'A Merrier Christmas'!" It was signed, "The Dayton Company."[4]

By 1936, the Dayton Company owned the whole block of Nicollet Avenue between Seventh and Eighth Streets. In 1937, the store announced that it would raise the Eighth Street building to ten stories and the Nicollet Corner to seven stories—improvements totaling $1 million. *Hennepin County Library.*

In 1932, George Dayton (right) received the honorary degree of Learned Doctor of Laws from Macalester College in St. Paul. *Hennepin County Library.*

Despite the economic struggles of that decade, Dayton's continued to expand. In December 1936, the company bought the land at the corner of Nicollet Avenue and Eighth Street, putting the entire block from Seventh to Eighth Streets under Dayton control.

"We are quite willing to have this purchase interpreted as an evidence of the faith of our 153 preferred and common stockholders in the future of Minneapolis and the Northwest," Nelson Dayton told the *Minneapolis Journal*.

The following March, Dayton's announced that it would raise the Eighth Street building to ten stories and the Nicollet Corner to seven stories—improvements totaling $1 million. Later that year, Nelson's eldest son, Donald, joined the store.

George Draper Dayton died on February 19, 1938, just before his eighty-first birthday. Headlines in the local papers lauded him as a "Leader in Northwest Business" and a "Pioneer in Building of Agriculture in Minnesota." The store was closed on February 21 for his funeral, which was held at

CASHIERS AT DAYTON'S LAUGH AT BANDIT

When a six-foot-tall bandit stepped up to a window in the Dayton Company's check-cashing bureau on April 28, 1932, and pointed a gun at the woman behind the store's new bulletproof glass demanding money, the cashier, Alice Schrader, laughed at him. "I haven't any," she said, according to a news report from the *Minneapolis Journal*.

The bandit then stepped over to the next cage and asked Olava Moose for money. She laughed, too, while stepping on the alarm button near her foot. The would-be robber fled, and clerk Louis Fogel followed him out of the store into a nearby alley, where the man turned to Fogel with the gun and said, "Get out of here."

Fogel did just that. Police scoured the area but never found the man.

Westminster Presbyterian Church and "was packed," according to his grandson Bruce Dayton. "When we got in the cars to go to Lakewood Cemetery, there seemed to me a sea of people standing at all the four corners of Twelfth Street and Nicollet. Hence I have always carried a clear impression of how highly respected in the community my grandfather was."[5]

Later reports in the local papers noted that he did not leave a large personal estate because of his lifetime "devotion of his accumulations

DAYTON'S ATHLETIC ASSOCIATION

Twenty years after the Dayton Company founded an athletic association for its employees, the group was still going strong in 1939. In October of that year, the *Minneapolis Times* ran a story about Dayton's Tuesday night bowlers ("Many a Dinner Is Missed by Dayton's Tuesday Bowlers"). The article claimed that more than eighty employee-bowlers skipped full-course dinners on bowling night, ate a light meal and hurried over to the Minneapolis Recreation alleys, where eight men's teams and eight women's teams spent an evening trying to knock down pins "for some fancy counts."

Although the bowling league was founded in 1920, women didn't join until 1936.

Each team used the name of the store department that the team members worked in, and the company gave prizes to the "most proficient" at the league's annual banquet in April.

As the newspaper reported, "Those 80-odd bowlers of the store look forward to their Tuesday nights. Come that evening they lose no time getting over to the alleys, even if it means the sacrifice of a good dinner."

One year later, the *Times* again reported on the store's athletic association and put the number of employees bowling at 120 in three leagues. The newspaper estimated that more than 350 Dayton's employees participated in some kind of sports through the store, including basketball, archery, rifle, table tennis, golf and tennis.

to philanthropic purposes. What he considered the most important achievement of his life was the giving of most of his personal fortune to the establishment of the Dayton Foundation."[6]

Chapter 7

War, Nylons and the Dayton Boys

Nelson Dayton's second son, Bruce Bliss Dayton, joined the company in 1940, just as the United States was moving out of the Depression and heading into World War II. Despite the uncertainty and turbulence of the time, the Dayton Company saw great growth and change in the 1940s.

Before the decade ended, all five of Nelson's sons were working in the company, the store had finished a $1.5 million expansion and customers saw the debuts of the Oval Room and the Studio of Interior Decorating and Designing. (The Studio, as it was called, was one of the first design studios to be placed in a department store. Its first attention-getting project was the penthouse apartment in the Hotel Radisson next door. The design of the new Town House quickly established the reputation of the studio, which sent buyers to Europe after the war to acquire furniture, Venetian glass and art objects from across the continent.)

Four of the Dayton sons served in the military during World War II. Donald, a Yale graduate who was the first to join the company in 1937, could not join the military because he had polio at the age of fourteen. Bruce, also a Yale graduate, had a brief stint in the war (Germany surrendered two days after he arrived in France). Wallace, an Amherst grad, served as a naval officer on a supply ship in the Pacific and then joined his father's store in 1946. Kenneth, a Yale graduate who served as a sergeant in General George Patton's tank corps, also joined the company in 1946. Douglas, the youngest, went to war in 1943, landed in France on D-Day, participated in the Battle of the Bulge and received a Purple Heart. He attended Amherst College after the war and joined Dayton's in 1948.

All five sons began their careers in Dayton's receiving room and learned how the merchandise came into the store. From there, they went to the stockroom and then to the sales floor.

In 1941, just months before Japan attacked Pearl Harbor, Dayton's announced that it would install "moving stairways" from the street floor to the fourth floor of the store. Most of the $300,000 Dayton's would invest into the new escalators would be spent in Minneapolis for wages and materials, the *Minneapolis Times* reported. The Minneapolis City Council changed parts of the city's building code to accommodate the project.

The Dayton Company celebrated its fortieth anniversary on January 20, 1942, the same way it marked its twenty-fifth anniversary in 1927: with a radio broadcast of the Minneapolis Symphony Orchestra. The hour-long concert was held at 9:15 p.m. and was broadcast on WCCO. It was exclusively a broadcast concert and was not open to the public.

The war had a curious effect on merchants like the Dayton Company. On one hand, buyers had a hard time obtaining goods to sell, but the scarcity of products guaranteed store sales. When store buyers couldn't obtain finished products, they found manufacturers to make the products for them. The store bought lumber or textiles—whatever was available—and contracted with new vendors to produce articles to order. Business was good, but it was different, as merchants found they had a new partner: the federal government.

When the Office of Price Administration was established to control inflation through the manipulation of commodity prices, merchants had the added burden of translating complicated pricing structures and the fear that a federal investigator could show up and find that regulations were not carried out.

MACHINE GUNS STOLEN IN DAYTON WINDOW BREAK

A Dayton's window display that featured guns on loan from author W.H.B. Smith to promote his new book, *How*, a manual on the use of small firearms, was broken into at about 3:45 a.m. on April 18, 1944.

The "thugs," as the article in the *Minneapolis Times* referred to the thieves, threw four heavy rocks through the plate glass and proceeded to take six weapons. The thieves knew what they were looking for, according to Detective Eugene Bernath. They took only guns for which U.S. regulation ammunition was available: a 1917 Lewis .30-06 light machine gun, two U.S. Reising .45-caliber submachine guns, a .38-caliber Smith & Wesson victory model revolver, a .38-caliber British service revolver and a .45-caliber navy revolver. They left behind a number of foreign, antiquated and ordinary guns such as a German machine gun, a British Hotchkiss tank gun and a British Bren light machine gun, as well as several Enfield and Springfield rifles.

Izetta Korems, an employee of the nearby Grand Café, was on her way home from work and walking down Seventh Street across from the store when she heard the glass crash. She looked up to see a large, dark car parked in front of the Dayton's window and then saw two men get out of the car, pull things from the window, dash back to the car, then back to the window and then to the car, the paper reported. Within seconds, the car pulled away and headed east on Seventh Street.

Dayton's night watchman, Andrew J. Wenzel, told police that he heard the glass crash, but by the time he had unlocked the door and gone outside, the car was driving away.

Minneapolis police chief Elmer F. Hillner issued a warning throughout the state that the thieves may use the stolen firearms to attempt bank holdups.

When the government initiated a scrap metal drive to increase resources for munitions in October 1942, Dayton's complied. Workers were sent to the roof of the building to dismantle the large "Dayton's" electric sign that had long lit up the sky with the company name.

When the U.S. Office of Defense Transportation announced that workday hours needed to be staggered to ease the overcrowding on streetcars and buses, the store complied again, sort of. The feds had asked department stores to change their workday hours to 10:00 a.m. to 6:00

Fashion Silhouettes

The Season's Silhouettes fashion show was presented on Friday, November 21, 1947, in the store's brand-new Sky Room, which had just opened the month before. The lunchtime show featured clothing to be worn "by candlelight," "in daylight," "at twilight," and "'neath moonlight" and included the following pieces:

By Candlelight
Café au lait crepe negligee, sequin-spattered—$35
Paris-inspired hostess coat in emerald taffeta—$35
Damian's ink-green velvet negligee sashed in cerise satin—$35

In Daylight
A coat of lustrous beaver with seven silvery stripes—$1,395
Paisley blue coat, pockets and yoke in black Persian lamb—$225
Ballerina suit, brown and beige checks above dark brown—$69.95

At Twilight
A mandarin neckline on a dress in charcoal grey—$49.95
A moiré apron is drawn over a black crepe dress—$35
A sequin and pearl necklace is embroidered on pearl grey crepe dress—$35

'Neath Moonlight
Florentine blue satin gown, the midriff traced in silver—$39.95
Light as mist gown of ice blue marquisette—$98.50
The windswept silhouette in whispering taffeta crimson gown—$335

---

p.m., but Dayton's felt that 6:00 p.m. seemed too late for its workers and 5:45 p.m. seemed much less so. Government officials were impressed with Dayton's assessment, and the store's hours throughout the war ran from 9:45 a.m. to 5:45 p.m., except on Mondays, when the store was open from noon to 9:00 p.m.

In 1943, the store ran ads announcing the shelving of many of its annual sales, including the September Jubilee Sale, which was canceled "to comply with the government agency's request that we have no promotion sales of textiles and textile products which comprise a major part of our merchandise."[1] In February 1944, Dayton's again ran ads apologizing for the cancelation of the Anniversary Sale.

Even without the sale, the store found a way to celebrate its forty-second anniversary and impress the crowds: Dayton's created a display of the area's history in miniature in its store windows along Nicollet Avenue. The display featured a scale model of the round tower at Fort Snelling in 1820, a view of St. Anthony Falls and the nearby lumber and flour mills in 1857, street scenes from 1885 and a view of Nicollet Avenue looking toward the old Westminster church, the site of what would become the Dayton Company.

"Dayton's had found a delightful way, Minneapolitans felt, of relating its own history to the history of the community," wrote James Gray in *You Can Get It at Dayton's.*[2]

Germany surrendered in May 1945, and by December of that year, Dayton's had announced that it would add five floors to the seven-floor corner at Nicollet and Eighth Street, extend the escalator service to the seventh floor and install air conditioning on all floors. Plans for the twelfth floor included the Sky Room Grill, conference rooms and an auditorium. Construction of a delivery building at 620 Olson Highway was also announced that year. The building was opened in May 1947. The facility housed ninety-two delivery trucks and some 130 employees, including drivers.

Launching an energetic expansion was news, but nothing said "the war is over" for the Dayton Company like the February 6, 1946 event that went down in the company's historical records as the "Battle of the Nylons."

Dayton's had been stocking nylons for months, until it had some ninety thousand pairs available—enough to make a "fair distribution among its customers."[3] And the store was aware that once these nylons were put on sale, it would attract thousands of shoppers.

Dayton's employees put together packages that contained two pairs each—the limit each customer could buy—and then locked them in the

Women jammed the floors of Dayton's for a chance to buy two pairs of nylon stockings in 1946. *Hennepin County Library.*

sub-basement fur vaults before the sale. The plan was to admit shoppers into the Eighth Street door and lead them by elevator to the third floor, where they would get into a queue that would make its way by escalator to the second floor. The customers would be led through the toy department, the boys' and menswear departments and the yard goods section, until they arrived at the cashiers' windows to pay for their nylons in advance. They would then take their receipt to the counters, where stockings were stacked by sizes and price.

The police department had agreed to send twenty-one officers to the store, and eight firefighters and the fire chief were on hand in case they were needed.

The streets surrounding Dayton's were filled by 6:30 a.m. on Wednesday, February 6, 1946, despite the cold and heavy snow—as well as a police alert that accused murderer George Sitts had just escaped from the Hennepin County Jail.

Nylon buyers had crowded the streets surrounding Dayton's by 6:30 a.m. on Wednesday, February 6, 1946, despite the cold and heavy snow. *Hennepin County Library.*

"Thousands of women and a considerable sprinkling of men, nylon-hungry, crowded into the Dayton Co. store today in one of the greatest buying rushes of the postwar era in Minneapolis," the *Minneapolis Times* reported. "Orderly and well-managed, the crowd lined up at all entrances

A postcard circa late 1940s or early 1950s of the outside of Dayton's. *Hennepin County Library.*

to the Dayton Company, in some instances jamming the street more than a block awaiting a chance to buy nylon stockings....Apparently thousands of Minneapolis husbands had been told to 'bring home my nylons.'"

The crowd was estimated at twenty thousand. The company had eighty-eight salespeople on hand working exclusively on the nylon sale. The store sold twenty thousand pairs that Wednesday and closed sales just after noon. The plan was to sell another twenty thousand pairs on Thursday and still another twenty thousand on Friday.

Minneapolis Star columnist Cedric Adams reported in his "Notes from the Nylon Front," dispelling one rumor that a baby had been born in the crowd and relaying anecdotes from the crowd (such as the woman who confided to a neighbor in line that she didn't know why she was there as she already had fifteen pairs of nylons at home).

On Saturday, February 9, Dayton's ran an ad announcing, "There will be no sale of stockings today."

Chapter 8

The Queen of the Oval Room

She always wore a black pearl in one ear and a white pearl in the other. They called her the Queen, Madame A and Mrs. A, and in the New York fashion market, she was the Merchant Princess.

Jeanne Auerbacher managed Dayton's downtown Minneapolis Oval Room from 1947 to 1956 and then moved on to develop Dayton's Little Couture Shop. She attempted to retire in 1961 but was asked to manage the Oval Room in St. Paul before she finally retired in 1964.

She was known as a buyer with impeccable taste and a saleswoman extraordinaire who counted as friends some of the great names in the fashion world during the 1930s and 1940s, including Gilbert Adrian (MGM Studio costume designer who created Judy Garland's gingham pinafore in *The Wizard of Oz* and established his own fashion house during the war), Hattie Carnegie (first to introduce ready-to-wear and launched many famous designers, including Norman Norell) and Philip Mangone (known as much for his elegant wool suits as his survival of the 1937 fire on the German passenger airship LZ 129 *Hindenburg* and its subsequent crash in New Jersey).

Born in Strasbourg, France, in 1898, Jeanne had a classical education and studied law before marrying William Auerbacher, who brought her to the United States in 1922. They settled in St. Paul, Minnesota, where William owned the largest broom-and-mop factory in the country. The business hit hard times during the Depression of 1929–32, and "he went broke," according to Margot Siegel, the Auerbachers' daughter.

The Oval Room label on a Ben Zuckerman coat, 1955–64. *Goldstein Museum of Design, gift of Audrae and Martin Diestler.*

Madame Jeanne Auerbacher. *Goldstein Museum of Design, gift of Margot Siegel.*

The demise of the business pushed Jeanne Auerbacher into looking for work. "She was a good friend of Elizabeth Quinlan of Young-Quinlan, the most beautiful store in the country in its day," Siegel said. "She asked if they had any room, and they put her behind the perfume counter. She was so great they moved her into one of the design departments. She sold clothes after that. Then everybody in the Twin Cities wanted her to work for them."

> MADAME A'S FASHION ADVICE
> FOR WOMEN OF A CERTAIN AGE
>
> The more elaborately you dress, the older you look.
> Never sacrifice dignity for youth. You should only look as young as your age allows.[1]

Auerbacher worked at a store called Raleigh's before moving on to Dayton's to sell sportswear in about 1934. She later worked for Stuart Wells in the Model Shop, the forerunner to the Oval Room.

The Model Shop began as the French Room, a department that carried a sampling of French designer clothes. After Germany declared war on France in 1939, French imports stopped, and Dayton's management renamed the venue the Model Shop and sold only American-made clothes.

"My mother was one of the people who made American designers important because she couldn't go to Europe because of the war, and she went out of her way to say how important American designers were," explained Siegel, who said she practically grew up in the fitting rooms at Dayton's. (Despite the Auerbacher family's economic woes, dressing well was not a problem for Siegel. "We were pretty poor," she said. "At one time they turned the lights out on us in our apartment. Although we had candles on the floor, I always wore designer clothes"—bought on markdown, of course.)

Siegel ended up with her own (unintentional) fashion career. A graduate of the University of Minnesota's journalism school, she was fashion editor for *Women's Wear Daily* in the late 1940s. ("I ended up on *Women's Wear* because the *New York Times* didn't hire me," she laughed. "When I was in journalism school, they said the worse thing that could happen to you is to end up on *Women's Wear Daily*. I loved working at it.") She wrote the book *Fashion (Looking Forward to a Career)*, published in 1974, and founded the Friends of the Goldstein Museum of Design, which provides volunteers, financial support and publicity for the University of Minnesota's design gallery. Many Twin Cities residents remember her for her pop-culture column "Margot" published in *Skyway News* in the 1990s.

STUART WELLS

Dayton's was the first department store to use a black model in fashion advertising when Erwin Blumenfeld photographed model Bani Yelverton for an Oval Room advertisement in *Vogue* in October 1958. Dayton's was the first to bring London's Youthquake fashions to the United States in the 1960s. Dayton's did many things first in the retail world, and most of those events were created by fashion expert Stuart Wells, who in 1938 was "lured from the fashionable Young-Quinlan store up the street," according to the book *The Birth of Target* by Bruce Dayton and Ellen Green.[2]

"He was very creative," said Dolores DeFore, who worked with Wells while a junior dress buyer at Dayton's in the 1960s. "He was probably too wild or too creative for Young-Quinlan. I heard stories of how they'd be pushing a rack of clothes, and he'd be hanging on the rack. Elizabeth Quinlan probably thought, 'This guy is too creative for me.'"

DeFore's take on how Wells got to Dayton's: "She sent him."

"He was a fabulous guy," Margot Siegel said. "He was a wonderful horseman, played polo. When my mother went into the Oval Room as a buyer, he was her merchandiser and later became president of the store. He did so many things first: the first to have flower shows for Easter and the Christmas shows and special weeks. He was one of the first to do the Youthquake, the first in America to do it."

Wells was also the first non-Dayton to be named president in the company. But seven months after stepping into that role, he died of a heart attack in December 1967. Just fifty-eight years old, Wells died while hunting at his farm in Sperryville, Virginia. An article printed in the *New York Times* on December 18, 1967, noted that Wells began his retail career as a salesman for Macy's in New York City and later for Bergdorf-Goodman.

When World War II ended, the Model Shop was remodeled and reopened in 1943 as the Oval Room, the brainchild of Wells. Auerbacher worked as his assistant until Wells was named divisional merchandise manager in 1947 and she took over.

"The Oval Room was beautiful, and it really was oval," Siegel said. "There were very few clothes out. You went into a fitting room, and they brought them to you. It was very fancy. In those days, only one store in the city would sell a designer, and now everybody sells everybody and everybody has the same stuff. It was a much more interesting time than it is now."

Judy Dayton bought her first piece from Madame Auerbacher in 1945, as she was about to leave for her freshman year at Connecticut College in New London, Connecticut. It was a green wool Davidow suit. She got to know Mrs. A, as she called her, when she returned to Minneapolis to marry Kenneth Dayton in 1953.

"She was awesome. She was really French and really bright and well read and witty," Dayton said. When one visited the Oval Room to buy clothes, "there was no merchandise visible. You'd sit in a room on a bench. They were quite nice big fitting rooms, and she would pick out stuff out of the stockroom. She would bring things in that she thought I would be interested in looking at." And she was "flawless at that," Dayton said. (She often wondered, though, what "fantastic" things were in the stockroom that they weren't showing her.)

Auerbacher had assistants who would run to the stockroom to get pieces of clothing she had instructed them to bring to the fitting room. "She had one assistant, her name was Robie, who would run back and forth from the fitting room to the stockroom," Dayton said. "On some days [Mrs. A] would say, 'Where is Robie?' and someone would say, 'Mrs. A, Robie has gone on break' or 'It's Robie's day off,' and [Mrs. A] would head to the stockroom herself and mutter, 'It's either her day off or her off day.' Poor old Miss Robie."

Despite the elegance of the Oval Room and its fitting rooms, as well as the no-smoking policy in those rooms, Auerbacher would light up her long, thin cigarettes as she worked with Judy Dayton. "You weren't supposed to smoke in the fitting rooms, but she did, so I did," Dayton said. Auerbacher smoked long, flat European cigarettes. Dayton smoked Chesterfields or Lucky Strikes. "I don't think you were supposed to smoke anywhere in the store, but there were ashtrays. It shows there was a flaw in their system," she laughed.

Auerbacher was fun to work with, Dayton said, but it was tiring. "It was a half-day expedition. She was exhausting but marvelous. She was a great merchant and a great salesperson and a good friend because she was really funny and helpful, and we were pals," Dayton said.

In the 1950s, the Dayton Corporation initiated a publicity campaign that attracted national attention. The company launched advertisements in magazines such as *Harper's Bazaar* and *Vogue*. It was rare to see a retailer outside of New York City advertising in those publications. Dayton's brought in nationally recognized photographers, including Erwin Blumenfeld, for its Oval Room ads. And the department held annual spring fashion shows and trunk shows that highlighted a designer's personal appearance.

"They would have a showing for two or three days when one of those designers came to town," Dayton said. "It was a big rumpus when that happened." One year, Bob Hope came to narrate a show.

After Auerbacher retired in the 1960s, the Oval Room began carrying European designers again. Madame A—who always wore black and a pillbox hat and carried an alligator handbag—died at age seventy-six in 1975.

THE MADAME'S PET PEEVE

Jeanne Auerbacher was a master saleswoman and a witty writer. In this undated selection from the papers of Jeanne Auerbacher—donated by Auerbacher's daughter, Margot Siegel, to the Goldstein Museum of Design at the University of Minnesota—the major-domo of the Oval Room for nearly two decades writes about a saleswoman's nuisance: the customer's girlfriend.

I have a pet peeve, the customer's girlfriend. By nature I am a peaceful person and I have nothing against girlfriends in general, but when they are taken along on shopping tours they arouse every sadistic instinct in me.

I had an experience the other day. In came a customer carrying a hatbox, which is a menace in itself. Are you curious as to why I have an aversion to hatboxes? It is because they invariably contain a hat that is supposed to be matched to a dress. But that was not enough, in also came friend Mabel, a very determined looking little person, and I knew more than one war was on.

Now back to the hatbox. I always play a silent guessing game before the box is opened. Will it be a green or a fuchsia hat? Women have a strange mania for buying green or fuchsia hats before they go to lunch and are determined to match their hats with dresses after they have had a chance to eat a hearty meal and gain in endurance and waistline. The hat was green.

Mabel helped to extract it from its many wrappings of tissue paper. She took it tenderly to the daylight so I could see its terrific greenness. Strange how colors can bring back incidents to your mind. I am not a seafaring person. The mal de mer *has spoiled more than one ocean trip for me. Anyhow, the hat was green and I was ready to have* mal de mer. *On top of the hat perched a bird, a yellow bird, a vicious little creature. It had a most superior look, as if it were going to say, "Just try and match me."*

There were exactly three green dresses in stock. I brought them in one by one with a feeling of pride and confidence, but I had not reckoned with Mabel. You see, Mabel had just had a permanent wave in a neighborhood beauty shoppe and while she sat under the dryer she had a chance to read every issue of Vogue *and* Mademoiselle *that had been published in the last six months. Her newly acquired knowledge had made her a self-appointed style dictator. She was actually part Mussolini and part Schapparelli.*

One of my dresses, she thought, was too much like last year's. She thought a little bustle would go so well with the bird on the hat. The second dress, she felt, was too youthful for Marion. And the third—I did not give her a chance to talk her friend out of my last dress. I knew I had to think and act quickly; strategy had to be used.

Meanwhile, the milk of human kindness had turned to dragon poison, but I am a saleswoman and every saleswoman must learn to be part Anthony Eden and part Clyde Beatty. With all my remaining patience, I concentrated on Mabel, only on Mabel.

I have a husband. The only way I can make him see things my way is to agree with his way. Why not try it on Mabel? I agreed with her. I agreed with everything, but I kept the third dress in reserve. Mabel was not used to having saleswomen agree with her. She always felt on the defensive. My complimenting her on her style knowledge took Mabel so completely by surprise that she suddenly became docile. (She even promised herself a subscription to Vogue!) *The third dress proved a success. Mabel won and so did I.*

But customer's girlfriends are my pet peeve.

Chapter 9

Birds, Art and Ten Acres of Shopping All Under One Roof

In April 1950, the Dayton brothers—Donald, Bruce, Kenneth, Wallace and Douglas—all under the age of thirty-six, took the reins of America's second-largest privately owned department store. Their father, Nelson, died of cancer in April and left each son 20 percent of the business. The brothers were joined by their cousin George D. Dayton II, Draper's son, who served as executive general manager.

It wouldn't take long for the new owners—who grew up on Blaisdell Avenue in Minneapolis just down the street from their grandfather, George Draper Dayton, and spent summers growing oats, hay and corn and raising prize-winning Guernseys and Belgian horses at their father's eight-hundred-acre Boulder Bridge Farm on Lake Minnetonka—to find that one department store wasn't big enough for all of them. Before the end of the decade, the company would buy department stores in Rochester (1954); Sioux Falls, South Dakota (1954); and St. Paul (1959) and make history with the 1956 opening of Southdale, the country's first enclosed, climate-controlled regional shopping mall.

Judy Dayton, the wife of Kenneth Dayton, remembered the mall's

> THE MISTERS
>
> Throughout the Dayton brothers' tenure with the business, everybody—starting just one layer down from top management—referred to them as Mr. Donald, Mr. Bruce, Mr. Wallace, Mr. Kenneth and Mr. Douglas.

Dayton's Minneapolis sold appliances until 1993 (this window display is from the 1950s). *Hennepin History Museum.*

An exterior view of Dayton's from the 1950s. *Hennepin County Library.*

A Revlon window display in 1955. *Hennepin History Museum.*

A postcard of Southdale in its early days. *Hennepin County Library.*

1954 groundbreaking in what she describes as a large, open hayfield. It was October, and as Bruce Dayton held his notes to give remarks, "the wind was blowing and the paper was fluttering. It was hard to hear what Bruce was saying. It was a field as far as the eye could see and I was standing there thinking, 'I can't imagine shopping here.'"

Southdale was opened to the public on October 8, 1956, and seventy-five thousand visitors did come to shop, or at least look, that day. The event was covered by *LIFE*, *Fortune*, *TIME*, *Women's Wear Daily*, the *New York Times*, *Business Week* and *Newsweek*. *TIME* called the mall a "pleasure-dome with parking."[1]

The mall had seventy-four stores with two three-story department stores anchored at each end of the mall: Dayton's was in the northwest corner, and Donaldson's (Dayton's lead competitor) was on the southeast corner.

The Daytons introduced the formula for regional shopping malls, according to Thomas Fisher, dean of the College of Design at the University of Minnesota. Southdale was "really a result of the Daytons realizing that there are only something like 120 good

THE MARGHAB SHOP

Despite Dayton's 1950s expansion into new communities, the brothers kept looking for ways to make the Minneapolis store the city's premier shopping experience—through advertising, special events and selling high-quality home furnishings, including Steuben glass, Orrefors crystal and Marghab Linens.

Emile Marghab Ltd. produced beautiful pieces of linen in Madeira, Portugal, and sold them only to stores selected by Vera Way Marghab (a South Dakota native) and her husband, Emile (a Cypress-born British citizen). The products—placemats, napkins, goblet rounds, handkerchiefs and more—were made of fine Irish linen and a crisp

A detail of a napkin embroidered in Madeira, Portugal, for Emile Marghab Ltd. *From the collection of Audrey Estebo.*

transparent fabric called Margandie, which was created in Switzerland for the company. The pieces were embroidered with thread hand-dyed in England and France, and the needlework was done in the homes of Madeira women who were paid by the stitch. Some of the pieces could contain as many as eighty-five thousand stitches.

Marghab began manufacturing in 1933, and its products were sold only in Madeira or to exclusive shops the Marghabs selected for their reputation for excellence and quality.[2] Those shops included Bullock's Wilshire in Los Angeles, Marshall Field's in Chicago, Nieman Marcus in Dallas, I.P. Magnin in San Francisco and Dayton's in Minneapolis.

Today, the linens are highly collectible, and many pieces belong in the permanent collection of the Metropolitan Museum of Art in New York City. A complete collection—1,918 pieces and 282 designs—is in the South Dakota Art Museum at Brookings.

We're Especially Proud of The Marghab Shop

One of the few shops in the whole world where you may see and buy the famous Marghab Collection of hand-embroidered Linens. Unequalled in fineness of quality, Marghab Linens have been the result of a tireless, unyielding effort to measure all parts of an organization to the same high standard. Colored linens from Ireland, exclusively-made sheer Margandie from Switzerland, original and distinctive designs—all these make Marghab Linens treasures to cherish as well as charming and inspiring accents to everyday living. Every piece is as fine as every other, from towels and dainty cocktail napkins to elaborate place-mat sets. Each design is a permanent member. Start a collection for yourself; introduce your friends with a gift.

A Dayton's holiday catalogue highlights the Marghab Shop. *Hennepin History Museum.*

shopping days a year in Minnesota," said Fisher. They knew an outdoor mall would greatly limit the desire for people to shop, "so they contacted Victor Gruen, an architect who had done [the Northland] outdoor mall in Detroit."

Gruen was born in Austria and spent his early years in Vienna, which had a lively pedestrian culture where people interacted on the streets and in shops and cafés. He was Jewish and fled Europe when the Nazis rose in power and ended up in New York, as the story goes, with just eight dollars in his pocket. He was charismatic and quickly became known as an interior store architect, Fisher said.

A socialist, Gruen was offended by the strip malls that had been dotting American suburbs and the social isolation created by suburban sprawl. He worried that people would go from their cars to their homes to their offices and never meet their neighbors. He envisioned "pedestrian precincts" in the communities, Fisher said. He wanted to create a town center where people would park their cars and go into a pedestrian environment where they interacted with one another. Gruen gave Southdale the same dimensions of a typical shopping street in Vienna.

The '50s was a decade when people dressed up to go shopping, Fisher said, and Southdale was meant to be a high-end experience. The new mall featured the Garden Court of Perpetual Spring, a large open space with a goldfish pond, an

HIGH-END HIGH ART

Southdale's high-end shopping experience was enhanced by the work of seven well-known contemporary artists who were commissioned to create pieces for the new shopping center.[3]

Italian-born Harry Bertoia created the mall's centerpiece, a forty-five-foot metal sculpture titled *Golden Trees*.

California artist Joseph Young created a mosaic mural of Byzantine glass for two exterior walls of a kiosk in the court.

Louise Kruger of New York created a laminated walnut carving of two boys, attached them to brass stilts and placed them in a planted area on the lower level of the center court.

The rest of the sculptures were made by Minneapolis artists. Dorothy Berge created *Unicycle*, a twelve-foot sculpture of copper and bronze depicting three clowns on a unicycle. Daniel Solerlin's nonobjective copper and bronze sculpture was fastened to the retaining wall at the entrance to Dayton's. Bernard Arnest painted a five- by ten-foot mural for the Southdale branch of the First National Bank. Dayton's restaurant, which was called Valley View Room at the time, held the six- by forty-one-foot mural by John Anderson.

The only piece that remains in Southdale is Bertoia's *Golden Trees*.

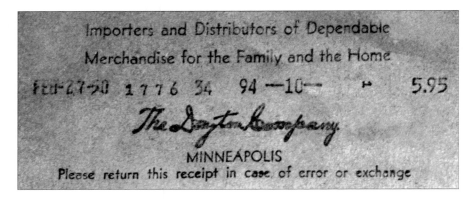

Importers and Distributors of Dependable
Merchandise for the Family and the Home
Feb-27-50   1776 34   94 —10—   ⊢   5.95
The Dayton Company.
MINNEAPOLIS
Please return this receipt in case of error or exchange

A 1950 receipt for a hat bought at Dayton's. *Hennepin History Museum.*

A Dayton's window display in October 1956. *Hennepin History Museum.*

aviary, sculptures by well-known artists, a sidewalk café and a stage to watch performances. Balls, banquets and a variety of events, including fine art exhibits and antique shows, were held there, and the mall catered to families with play areas, a small zoo in the basement and a childcare area where parents could drop off their children while they shopped.

NAME CHANGE

Cedric Adams wrote the following in his November 15, 1953
Minneapolis Tribune *column "In this Corner."*

You'll see some changes tomorrow and I think they'll amaze you. The Dayton Company is changing its name. Don't be too alarmed, however, the change isn't drastic. Ask anybody you meet what the name of the store on Eighth and Nicollet is and they'll tell you it's Dayton's. Through the years, almost everybody has referred to the store that way, including the Dayton people themselves. Starting tomorrow, then, the Dayton Company becomes simply "Dayton's." Even the old Dayton signature will die and a new "logo" will start appearing in ads, displays and wherever the firm name is used....

You don't make a switch like this over night. A lot of intensive research went into the design of the store's new signature. It took Dayton's publicity heads three weeks of night-and-day sessions, which started last August, to come up with a finished product. Prior to that, the idea had been months in the mulling-over process. A store signature must be adaptable to a variety of uses, from newspaper ads to delivery trucks and a thousand places in between....

Makes you wonder how many of us will be around when the next Dayton change is made.

The Dayton's label reflects the company's change from the Dayton Company to just Dayton's.

"MEET YOU AT THE AIR DOOR"

In 1959, Dayton's installed a "modern air door"—a nineteen-foot-wide "curtain of air" that directed air downward to a grill on the floor, where the air was filtered, heated or cooled and then recirculated by fans. The moving air insulated the interior of the store from outside dust, dirt, snow, rain, temperatures, animals and insects, the store claimed in a 1959 advertisement. At night and on weekends, the store secured the entrance with a sliding door.

Pam Albinson, who was a member of Dayton's Teen Board in 1960–61, said the Seventh Street door was a popular landmark and meeting place: "If a car was going to pick you up, you'd say, 'Meet you in two hours at Dayton's Seventh Street air door.'"

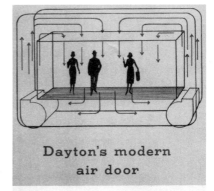

Dayton's modern air door

It's a 19-foot wide curtain of air directed downward to a grille on the floor, where the air is filtered, washed, heated or cooled and re-circulated by fans. The moving curtain of air, which resembles a waterfall, insulates the interior of Dayton's from outside dust, dirt, snow, rain, temperatures, animals and insects. The air door presents a completely unobstructed opening into the store. Nights and week-ends, when Dayton's is closed, sliding doors secure the entrance.

Dayton's Modern Air Door was a popular landmark. *Hennepin History Museum.*

Southdale is a "terrific example of how the Daytons were thinking of ahead of their time," Fisher said. "They weren't afraid of trends. Part of their success was to go with new ideas and not worry about whether a new idea might undercut an old idea. Part of the risk, of course, was that Southdale would drain its downtown store of business. ...They never seemed to back away from doing things, even when it put other aspects of their business at risk. That is a big part of why they were successful."

The Dayton brothers' willingness to take chances was exemplified when they came up with the idea of placing two competing department stores at

The Dayton brothers. *Left to right*: Douglas, Wallace, Donald, Kenneth and Bruce. *Target Corp.*

each end of a shopping center. "Typically, a department store would fund these things, so they would have noncompeting smaller stores around [the main department store]," Fisher said. "The Daytons had the idea of putting in the competitor, in this case Donaldson's, so it would attract more people."

Gruen was involved in the design of the Daytons' subsequent shopping centers—Brookdale in Brooklyn Center (1966), Rosedale in Roseville (1969) and Ridgedale (1974) in Minnetonka—as well as the building of the new downtown St. Paul store in 1963.

The success of Southdale and other malls designed by Gruen launched a wave of covered malls in the country. More than eight thousand new shopping malls were opened in the United States between 1960 and 1970. Initially, Gruen thought that he had found the formula for conquering urban sprawl, but in the end, he found he'd contributed to it, said Fisher.

The architect envisioned shopping centers as the core of more vibrant communities, with houses, apartments, schools and offices surrounding them. He was disappointed that his ideas weren't fully embraced, and in 1964, he refocused his architectural practice on revitalizing downtowns through the creation of pedestrian malls.

Gruen returned to Vienna in the late 1960s and retired shortly after that. In 1978, Dayton's left the mall business, selling Southdale and eight other malls to the Equitable Life Assurance Society of the United States for $305 million in cash and debt.[4]

Chapter 10

The Eighth-Floor Extravaganzas

J ack Barkla can still picture the animated circus that "went from window to window to window" at Dayton's during a Christmas season when he was a child. Visiting the Dayton's holiday displays was a big event for Barkla, who grew up in Minneapolis in the 1940s and '50s. "I remember as a child going down there with my relatives. We'd always go down to see the Dayton's windows," he said. "There was something totally magic about it. I got that." Yes, he did.

Sometime in the late 1960s—he can't quite remember the year—Barkla began creating his own magic on Dayton's eighth floor when he was hired to paint backdrops and later design sets for the store's Christmas and spring flower shows.

Dayton's was known for its elaborate Christmas show windows from its start, but after the company's Edina shopping mall, Southdale, opened in 1956, management became concerned that suburban families would drive by the store windows after they were unveiled on Thanksgiving but skip going into the store to shop. Bringing some seasonal extravaganza into the store was a way to thank the public for shopping at Dayton's and also entice shoppers onto the sales floors.

"Originally, the flower shows and Christmas shows were relegated to the first floor," Barkla said. "They'd clear out all the retail and build their gardens." In 1963, the shows moved to the eighth-floor auditorium, and Dayton's put most of its Christmas promotional budget toward the eighth-floor shows.

Dayton's Christmas windows in 1923. *Hennepin County Library.*

A Christmas window display from 1940. *Hennepin History Museum.*

In 1967, *Dickens' London Towne* cost as much as a ten-year run of holiday windows, but it also brought 30,000 visitors into the store the day after Thanksgiving and 110,000 visitors through the show's run.[1]

Barkla, who studied art at the University of Minnesota and scene design under composer Richard Wagner's granddaughter, Friedelind Wagner, in Nuremberg, Germany, has a résumé that includes set design at the Minnesota Opera, Loyce Houlton's dance company, the Guthrie Theater and the Children's Theatre Company. His first full show at Dayton's was in 1973: *The Nutcracker.*

"I studied opera in Germany, and I thought this was wonderful," Barkla said. "I knew Nuremberg, and I remembered standing outside [Renaissance painter] Albrecht Dürer's home in the rain in Nuremberg, and I decided, 'Let's do it in Nuremberg style of architecture.'"

Barkla designed *The Nutcracker* at Dayton's again in 1997. This time, it was Maurice Sendak's version of the story. When Barkla was told that he would be designing dozens of sets using Sendak's work, he was concerned about how to re-create the illustrator's scenes.

The 1966 eighth-floor holiday show was *Dickens' Village* (above). The next year, Dayton's displayed *Dickens' London Towne. Hennepin County Library.*

DICKENS' LONDON TOWNE '67

This page and next: In 1967, *Dickens' London Towne* brought thirty thousand visitors into the store the day after Thanksgiving. *Hennepin County Library.*

Awaiting you . . . these special Christmas features at Dayton's!

Christmas Kid-Doodles, an excitingly new book for children designed expressly by Dayton's and filled with fun and games, Dickens' style. You'll find it for sale in the Amelia Martin Millinery Shop, Augustus Cooper's Oil and Color Shop (London Towne) and in our 4th Floor Santa Land.

Santa Land, this year in a brand new location on the 4th Floor. Here the children may talk with Santa, have their picture taken with him and receive a free Christmas crown. Kid-Doodles books for sale here.

The "For Children Only Shop," now located in Dickens' London Towne and going under the name of "The Gruff & Tackleton Shop!" No parents allowed. All gifts are modestly priced to fit tiny budgets!

Gabriel Parsons' Sugar-Baker Shop, where you'll find tempting old fashioned sugar and ginger cookies . . . 2 for 5¢ right out of the barrel! Plus a delightful array of penny candy displayed in old-time apothecary jars. All treats are for sale!

A brief biography on London Towne's Charles Dickens

Charles Dickens . . . born on the 7th of February, 1812 . . . was the son of a Naval Pay Officer. His childhood was poverty-stricken and at 12 he was hard at work in a blacking warehouse. He never attended a regular school until 1821 and claimed his first desire for knowledge and reading were awakened by his mother.

He started his hand at writing as a court and parliamentary reporter, followed by magazine articles and short stories. No incident in his life seemed to pass him by and many of his experiences found their place in his writings. A considerable number were children-oriented and perhaps this is due to the fact that he himself had 10!

From the authentic English lights to our own cobblestone streets, we have tried to capture the feeling of the Dickens' era and highlight some of his fascinating characters. It is with pleasure Dayton's presents DICKENS' LONDON TOWNE '67.

Above: Jack Barkla's drawing of one of the scenes from *The Grinch*, Dayton's holiday show in 1998. *Courtesy of Jack Barkla.*

Left: A scene from the 1998 holiday show, designed by Jack Barkla. Sculptures were created by Dan Mackerman. *Courtesy of Jack Barkla.*

THE EIGHTH-FLOOR
CHRISTMAS SHOWS

1963: *Santa's Enchanted Forest*
1964: *Land of Trolls*
1965: nameless; animated
    animals preparing for
    Christmas
1966: *Dickens' Village*
1967: *Dickens' London Towne*
1968: *Under the Giant Christmas Tree*
1969: *Peter Pan*
1970: *Santa's Toy Workshop*
1971: *Santa's TV Studio*
1972: *Joy to the World* (Joan Walsh
    Anglund)
1973: *The Nutcracker*
1974: *Grandma Moses' "Christmas in the
    Country"*
1975: *'Twas the Night Before Christmas*
1976: *Charlie and the Chocolate Factory*
1977: *How the Grinch Stole Christmas*
    (Dr. Seuss)
1978: *Once Upon a Christmastime*
1979: *Babes in Toyland*
1980: *Alice's Wonderland Christmas*
1981: *Hansel and Gretel*
1982: *Pippi Longstocking*
1983: *Babar and Father Christmas*
1984: *Animalen, "The Peaceable
    Kingdom"*
1985: *The Velveteen Rabbit*
1986: *Santabear's First Christmas*
1987: *Santabear's High-Flying
    Adventures*
1988: *The Polar Express*
1989: *Cinderella*

"There are these magnificent illustrations [in Sendak's book], and there were almost no environments—figures alone and maybe one or two different environments," Barkla said. "I told the people at Dayton's, 'I'm not going to do it unless I talk to Maurice. I have to make up scenes in his style and his name goes on this, and I don't want to do anything he doesn't approve of.' And they said, 'Nobody talks to Maurice. *Nobody* talks to Maurice.' Then I said, 'I'm not doing it.'"

In the end, Barkla did talk to Maurice at Sendak's home in Connecticut. One of Barkla's tasks was to get more information about the strange rocky caves that Sendak had illustrated in the book's Candyland scene.

Few people know what the Nutcracker story represents, Barkla explained. "The original story by E.T.A. Hoffman is about the sexual maturing of a young girl. Maurice, a man of great integrity, believed in telling the story as E.T.A. Hoffman intended."

It turns out that Sendak's Candyland caves represented, well, female anatomy. When Barkla returned to Minneapolis and relayed that information at a planning meeting, "there was total silence in the room, and after about five seconds one man looks at his watch and says, 'Oh, I'm late for another meeting,' and that room was empty in about two and a half minutes."

Later, Barkla said he assured the store's management "that when I did the show I would try to honor both Maurice's desires and the E.T.A. Hoffman story and make sure that there's enough of our idealized version of 'The Nutcracker' so that people who expect that will also have that. I think we hit a mark with that."

For many years, Barkla and the team who created these shows chose the subjects. "To this day those were the most well-attended shows we had. We did 'Christmas Carol'; we did 'Puss and Boots'; we did 'Cinderella'—two different 'Cinderellas'—'Wind in the Willows.' Those were some of our best-attended shows. It helps to have the people that build it be in on the original conception of it."

Painter and sculptor Dan Mackerman recalled his second show, *Cinderella*, in 1989: "The thing that was cool about that work is everything was experimental. We were constantly inventing things for the job. I started out as a painter, but in those days, a need would arise, a job would come across our table and we would find the easiest, quickest way to do it."

During the making of *Cinderella*, Mackerman was asked if he would construct the carriage: "I had never sculpted before. I went through a ton of tools figuring out how to do this." In the end, the giant pumpkin carriage was made of Styrofoam, a product that became the medium of choice for many of the large stationary three-dimensional pieces of the shows—all of which were created on the eighth floor.

1990: *Peter Pan*
1991: *Pinocchio*
1992: *Puss in Boots*
1993: *Beauty and the Beast*
1994: *The Wizard of Oz*
1995: *The Wind in the Willows*
1996: *A Christmas Carol*
1997: *The Nutcracker* (Maurice Sendak)
1998: *How the Grinch Stole Christmas*
1999: *The 12 Days of Christmas*
2000: *Harry Potter*
2001: *'Twas the Night Before Christmas* (Marshall Field's)
2002: *Paddington Bear and the Christmas Surprise* (Marshall Field's)
2003: *Charlie and the Chocolate Factory* (Marshall Field's)
2004: *Snow White* (Marshall Field's)
2005: *Cinderella* (Marshall Field's)
2006: *Mary Poppins* (Macy's)
2007: *The Nutcracker* (Macy's)
2008: *A Day in the Life of an Elf* (Macy's)

Dan Mackerman with his sculptures from *The Wind in the Willows* (1995), Maurice Sendak's *The Nutcracker* (1997) and *A Christmas Carol* (1996). *Dan Mackerman.*

One of the many expressions of Scrooge. *Kristal Leebrick.*

Charlie and the Chocolate Factory, designed by Jack Barkla. *Dan Mackerman.*

"In those days you could work twenty-four hours if you wanted," Mackerman said. "You could work all night, and I did."

After Mackerman created the thirty-foot (Styrofoam) whale for *Pinocchio*, he became known as a sculptor, and it wasn't long before he began sculpting all the figures for the shows.

"They were getting these figures from New York City, and they were just duller than dull," he said. "They did *Beauty and the Beast*, and they had used some mold in which the mold slipped and the corner of Beauty's mouth looked like she had Bell's palsy. That was the year Jack Edwards, the costume designer, came up to me and asked if I would be interested in sculpting all the figures for the show. *Christmas Carol* was the first year I was allowed to just go nuts on the facial expressions. I had five different facial expressions for Scrooge."

The shows included the elaborate work of Jack Edwards, a costume designer who was known in the Twin Cities for his work with the Guthrie, pianist Lorie Line's holiday tours and even a show by Prince. Edwards began

THE STONEWORK WAS LOVELY

One of Jack Barkla's favorite Dayton's-Bachman's flower shows was the 1991 Fiori D'Italia—"a *Reader's Digest* condensed tour of Italian gardens," he told Mary Abbe at the *Star Tribune*. The show featured a cascade of water tumbling through a series of basins into a pool along with seventeen fountains and water jets, a Temple of Apollo with statues representing the four seasons, benches, frescoes, vine-draped pergolas and two loud macaws in an aviary in the middle of the piazza. It also featured the eighth-floor artists' signature Styrofoam, which was carved and painted to look like marble, granite and even lichen-covered rock.

The brochure cover from the 1994 spring flower show. *Hennepin County Library.*

Dayton's and Bachman's

Spring Flower Show

F L O R E S

M E X I C A N A S

March 18 to April 2, 1994

Dayton's Minneapolis

8th floor Auditorium

his career on Broadway in New York and then designed in Hollywood for television shows, including *The Carol Burnett Show* and *The Jim Nabors Show*. He died in January 2013 at the age of seventy-eight.

Sally Glassberg Sands, director of special events at Dayton's in the 1980s, described Barkla as a genius. "Barkla and Edwards were an extraordinary team and created magnificent auditorium events," she said. "They never disappointed. It was a privilege to work with artists of such talent, imagination and integrity. It was an education and an honor to talk with Barkla about his vision since it always reflected so much heart and soul and deep understanding of both the story and the audience."

Each show took five to eight months to plan, Barkla said. "As soon as the flower show opened, we would have the theme for the Christmas show, and I would do preliminary floor plans."

It took a lot of trial and error to figure out traffic flow (Americans love to go counterclockwise in any exhibit, Barkla said. "If you do it clockwise, you don't get many people through because they slow up. In Europe and Asia, it's just the opposite.") and detail ("People are fascinated by detail. In *Wind in the Willows*, the picnic had all these kinds of cakes spread out, and we had a line of ants going across the blanket and then up attacking the food.").

Barkla claimed that he was not quite three when he was pointed in the direction of set design. "My mother took me to see a Fred Astaire film called *Daddy Long Legs*. In the movie, Fred Astaire, through different camera work and so on, dances with himself, and you see many images. I asked my mother how they did that and she said, 'Mirrors.' I was just really intrigued by this illusion of something."

THERE WAS ALWAYS SOMETHING TO
SEE AT DAYTON'S

Dayton's had a history of presenting interesting exhibits to the public. In 1934, the store hosted an agricultural panorama that displayed the detailed process of moving grain from the fields to grain elevators to freight cars and ships, and finally to flour mills. The exhibit was set up on the fourth floor of the Dayton Company store.

The "model of the machinery of modern grain marketing," created by the Farmers' National Grain Corporation, was fresh from the Chicago Century of Progress exhibit. The display included a forty-foot field of grain and an electric train with an engine and grain cars that moved through the grain field to a working model of a mill and elevator. Another part of the exhibit displayed models of the mill and elevator plans for General Mills and a one-hundred-year-old grain reaper made by Cyrus H. McCormick.

On an April morning in 1965, the eighth floor set the stage for a circus with three elephants, fifteen ponies and five poodles, along with a few seals and leopards borrowed from the Como Zoo in

St. Paul. John Herriott, an animal trainer from Circus World in Baraboo, Wisconsin, encountered a number of flooded roads en route to Minneapolis and arrived at Dayton's five hours late. The Como animals were on loan, just in case he didn't show up.

In 1972, a much smaller circus was on display on the eighth floor: the Dunn Bros. Circus, made up of more than 1 million handmade intricately carved pieces that included more than twenty thousand miniature performers and spectators, 1,000 horses, 277 elephants, 80 camels and seventy-seven tents. The circus was displayed on a three-thousand-square-foot table and used more than seven hundred tiny electric lights.

The miniature circus was also animated, and Harry Dunn, the circus's creator, was able to re-create 140 circus acts through the use of electronic animation.

Both Barkla and Mackerman still work on the eighth floor for special events at what is now Macy's. The store has continued the partnership with Bachman's floral company to host the spring flower show, and since 2008, Macy's Christmas show has been *A Day in the Life of an Elf*, which both artists helped create.

Chapter 11

The Swingingest Spot in Minneapolis

D ayton's set a course for rapid change in the mid-1950s with the opening of Southdale and stores in Rochester, St. Paul and South Dakota, and it moved into the 1960s ready for more.

In May 1962—the same year Kmart opened in Garden City, Michigan, and Walmart debuted in Rogers, Arkansas—the Dayton Company opened its first Target on Snelling Avenue in Roseville, Minnesota. By the end of the year, Target stores were opened in Duluth and the Twin Cities suburbs of St. Louis Park and Crystal.

Target was the Dayton Company's reaction to the discount-merchandising trend gaining speed in the United States. Selling less expensive merchandise to more customers meant more profit than catering to a smaller crowd that could pay more.[1] Douglas Dayton was the lead in the new venture.

This was the decade when the company would shed its longstanding aversion to conducting commerce on Sundays and serving liquor in its restaurants. In 1964, the company opened two of its Target stores on Sundays and launched a study in 1967 to assess the "feasibility" of opening its department stores on Sundays. In 1968, Dayton's twelfth-floor Minneapolis restaurants, the Sky Room and Oak Grill, got liquor licenses.

Minneapolis Star columnist Jim Klobuchar welcomed the new department store amenity in his column: "Dayton's thus becomes one of the few general stores in the territory that can sell screwdrivers not only from its eighth-floor hardware department but also from its twelfth-floor kitchen."

DAYTON'S TEEN BOARD

Dayton's recruited senior high school girls from across the Twin Cities metro area in the 1960s to serve on its Teen Board. Thirty girls from twenty-six public schools and four private schools spent their senior years working as salespeople in the store's Young Junior Department, staging fashion shows and serving as a great public relations tool that encouraged other teens to buy clothes at the store.

Pam Albinson, Anoka High School's Teen Board representative in 1960–61, caught a bus after school on the afternoons she worked in the store and took it downtown. She did her homework on the sometimes hour-long bus ride because she worked until 9:00 p.m. and then took the bus back to Anoka.

Although she worked hard that year, Albinson said that it was an honor to be on the board. "You have no idea how absolutely thrilled I was. It was thrilling because Dayton's treated us so well."

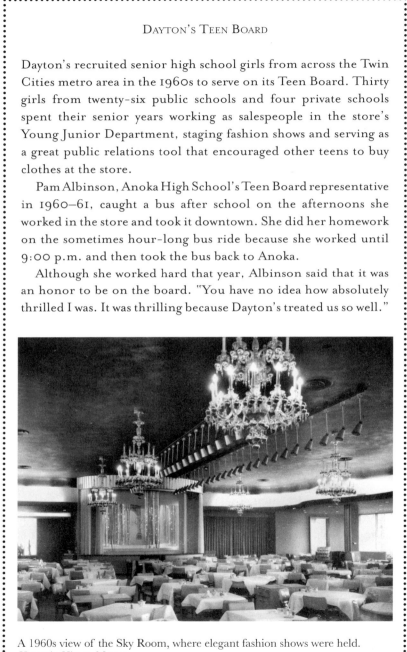

A 1960s view of the Sky Room, where elegant fashion shows were held. *Hennepin History Museum.*

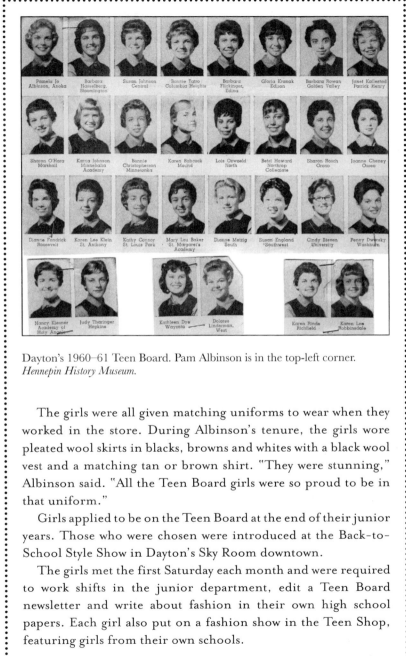

Dayton's 1960–61 Teen Board. Pam Albinson is in the top-left corner. *Hennepin History Museum.*

The girls were all given matching uniforms to wear when they worked in the store. During Albinson's tenure, the girls wore pleated wool skirts in blacks, browns and whites with a black wool vest and a matching tan or brown shirt. "They were stunning," Albinson said. "All the Teen Board girls were so proud to be in that uniform."

Girls applied to be on the Teen Board at the end of their junior years. Those who were chosen were introduced at the Back-to-School Style Show in Dayton's Sky Room downtown.

The girls met the first Saturday each month and were required to work shifts in the junior department, edit a Teen Board newsletter and write about fashion in their own high school papers. Each girl also put on a fashion show in the Teen Shop, featuring girls from their own schools.

> "Dayton's helped us learn how to do a style show," she said. "We picked our clothes. We had a theme. We picked our own models from our own schools. We did our own public relations, and we picked our own music and entertainment for the show."
>
> Albinson's show was held in October, just before Halloween, which was fitting as Albinson's hometown of Anoka calls itself the "Halloween Capital of the World." The October fashion show took on a Halloween theme, Albinson said. "I barely remember it, except that I know that working on it was a genuine thrill."

By 1968, Southdale and Brookdale—and the Dayton's stores that anchored the two malls—were keeping the doors open on Sundays.

The Daytons knew that both their downtown store and downtown Minneapolis itself needed to change to keep shoppers in the city center. Donald Dayton, the company president in the first half of the decade, championed the building of the downtown skyway system—an eleven-mile network of enclosed second-story sidewalks that gave pedestrians a milder way to traverse downtown during cold weather. He also campaigned to create an open-air pedestrian mall on Nicollet Avenue.

In 1966, the Nicollet Mall—which runs between Fifth and Twelfth Streets—broke ground. The mall opened in October 1967, complete with trees, benches and an eighteen-foot-high, 1,500-pound sculpture by Alexander Calder, commissioned by Dayton's at an estimated cost of $50,000. The store itself was remodeled so that passersby could look directly into boutiques rather than just at window-display mannequins. Inside, the cultural upheaval of the 1960s was making its way into the merchandise.

Dolores DeFore recalled the day her boss, Stuart Wells—the vice-president of merchandising and publicity who would eventually become the first non-Dayton president of the store—told her that she needed to head to London. Fast. "[He] came back from Europe in May and said, 'Dolores, you've got to go to London now.'"

Within a week, DeFore had landed at Heathrow Airport and began a tour of the British city, the epicenter of the "Youthquake" fashion movement. She toured the trendy boutiques on Carnaby Street and the showrooms of designers Mary Quant, Angela Cash and Gerald McCann. Skirts were short, and so were the hairstyles.

"[The clothes] were so cute, and they looked cute on everybody," DeFore said. "They were so much shorter than clothes being sold in the States. They were quite simple A-line shapes, and once somebody put one of those on, they wanted to come back for two or three more dresses. It was such a change in fashion. We were so conservative compared to what was over there."

By the end of her stay, she had signed up Cash, Quant and McCann to come to Minnesota.

DeFore—who was a buyer for Junior Dresses at the time—brought the "London Look" to Minneapolis that August for a month-long back-to-school promotion, "Super Youthquake." The month's events included fashion shows (with live music and dancing models) and concerts by national artists Simon and Garfunkel, the Chad Mitchell Trio and the Yardbirds. The store even got a Beatles look-alike band from Liverpool to come and play each day in the junior department.

"It was phenomenal," she said. "We beat the New York stores. Dayton's was the first one." Other stores—including Bloomingdale's and Abraham & Straus in New York—set their London promotions for September.

That month, *Newsweek* called Dayton's the "swingingest spot

ART AND THE COLD WAR

In June 1967, Dayton's hosted the first Moscow-approved show and sale of contemporary Russian art outside the Soviet Union since World War II. The show met with cries of treason by some area residents. More than a dozen demonstrators stood for seven hours outside the department store to protest the exhibit when it opened. The group wore black armbands and small American flags and carried signs denouncing "this wicked trade" with the Soviet Union.

A photo printed in the *Minneapolis Tribune* showed signs that read, "Moscow approved Dayton sale of Bolshevik 'art,'" and, "If you believe trade with reds is treason, join us!" The protestors were from a group called Christian Research Inc.

The art show, held in the eighth-floor auditorium, was from a four-hundred-piece collection of art imported by Milwaukee millionaire Henry L. Carlsruh. The collection consisted mostly of landscapes, still-life paintings and portraits that ranged in price from $10,000 for an oil portrait by an artist named Falk to $200 for a carved stone chess set from a region near Mongolia.

Dayton's told the newspaper that Carlsruh had purchased the artwork from a Soviet government export agency that fed the proceeds of purchases back to the artists. The money from the sale of the art in Minneapolis would go directly to Carlsruh.

The protests didn't stop people from viewing the show, according to another report from the *Minneapolis Tribune* two days later. A subsequent show scheduled to open in Milwaukee on June 12 was canceled, however. The reasons for the cancelation were described as "political, esthetic and technical."[3]

in Minneapolis." Speaking at an October Minnesota Retailers Federation meeting, Wells described the effect the country's youth was having on his store's merchandising methods: "The young are starting changes. The wealthy of Paris and London used to set the fashion, but today it may be among the young and poor in Liverpool."[2]

DeFore would later become merchandising manager for the Oval Room and eventually leave Dayton's to run Harold— an upscale women's clothing store in Minneapolis—with Robert Dayton, son of Donald Dayton, but she remembered that time in the juniors department as great fun.

"I was in the right place at the right time," she said.

The spring after the Super Youthquake promotion, a wispy British teenager came to Dayton's. It was the only department store that supermodel Twiggy visited on her trip to the United States that year and the only stop she made outside of New York. A crowd of 1,500 mostly teenage girls came to the eighth-floor auditorium to see the skinny seventeen-year-old on April 23, 1967.

When Twiggy arrived at the Minneapolis–St. Paul airport the day before, three hundred fans were waiting there along with eight very thin Minneapolis teens made up in Twiggy fashion and holding silver "Welcome Twiggy" signs. Dayton's had begun advertising for "Twiggys" the month before. The qualifications: five feet, six inches tall, ninety-one pounds and a bust size of thirty-one inches, waist of twenty-two and hips of thirty-two.

One story that made the papers was a tale of three teens who bluffed their way into a carefully restricted press conference at an airport pressroom. The girls, Cheryl Halverson, Kathy Frommer and Carol Croonquist—editors of the Bloomington Lincoln High School *Mah-Que*—flashed red cards that read, "Press," and joined reporters from *LIFE*,

DAYTON'S TOP TEN CLUB

One of Dayton's most well-attended promotions in the mid-1960s was its Saturday afternoon teen dances in the eighth-floor auditorium, Dayton's Top Ten Club. The dances were hosted by radio station WDGY (or WeeGee) disc jockey Bill Diehl and featured live bands. It attracted so many teens that the store had to set a limit on attendance at 1,200.

Sarah Massey attended those dances as a junior high school girl from south Minneapolis. Every Saturday, she and her best friend, Jenny, dressed in white Levis and cranberry T-shirts, took a bus downtown and waited for boys to ask them to dance. "They never did, so we would dance with each other," she said. "We were twelve, which is why we never got asked to dance. There were *real* girls there."

The auditorium was kept dim, and folding chairs lined the walls. ("That's where you'd go and sit, if your heart wasn't totally broken," Massey said.) The show hosted live bands from the area, including the Castaways, whose song "Liar, Liar" hit no. 12 on the Billboard Hot 100 in 1965. "It was always very well attended, and it was free. It was a great thing for young teenage kids to be able to go to and see live bands," Massey said.

In 1966, a Minneapolis police spokesperson suggested that Dayton's shut down the dances after a fight broke out on January 22. A fourteen-year-old boy was beaten and kicked as he and three companions were leaving the dance. The same day, a store security officer was attacked while trying to control a crowd of about one hundred teens on the fifth floor.

After the disturbance, rumors spread that the dances would be canceled because none had been scheduled through February. But on March 1, Dayton's announced that it was expanding its teen dances by bringing in nationally famous musicians for some of them. The following August, the store launched its back-to-school promotion "Super Youthquake," which included concerts by the Yardbirds, Simon and Garfunkel and the Chad Mitchell Trio.[4]

the *Milwaukee Journal* and all the local media. After the press conference, Frommer told a *Minneapolis Star* reporter that she thought the hysteria of the crowd was "ridiculous. People are so stupid to idolize an ordinary, everyday teenager just like us. If I were her, I'd wonder how people can be so taken in."

GUN (SALES) CONTROL

In the 1960s, Dayton's sold refrigerators, stoves, washers and dryers; had a hardware department stocked with power drills, belt sanders and assorted sizes of ladders; and sold sporting goods, including canoes, fishing equipment and guns.

In 1968, several Twin Cities retailers—Donaldson's, Sears and Montgomery Ward—announced that they would no longer sell firearms through mail order or over the phone. In response, Dayton's told the *Minneapolis Tribune* that "it never has accepted mail or phone orders for guns or ammunition" and that the store "will continue to keep records of all firearms purchased."

A Dayton's spokesman told the newspaper that the store adhered "to all local ordinances governing the sale of firearms. When no local gun-control rulings exist, we require that the buyer of a rifle or shotgun be at least eighteen years of age," and "a buyer must be twenty-one to purchase a handgun."

Dayton's advertised guns and ammunition only at the opening of hunting season, the spokesperson said. "Dayton's has not and will not advertise handguns," but the store had no plans at that time to discontinue the sale of them.

Just two days before the article appeared, Donaldson's had announced that it would no longer advertise firearms and that it was discontinuing the mail-order sale of guns. The store also announced that it had discontinued the sale of handguns completely three weeks prior.[5]

Dayton's kept up with fashion and cultural trends throughout the decade: holding yoga workshops; bringing in an astrologer, who set up a computerized horoscope service in the store and predicted that in 1969 researchers would reveal that the cure for cancer was partly psychological; screening two collections of experimental films by directors such as Francois Truffaut and Roman Polanski; launching B. Dalton, Bookseller; and opening Gallery 12 on the twelfth floor, a contemporary art gallery that sold Tom Wesselmann nudes, Robert Rauschenberg lithographs and sculptures by Marisol Escobar.

SOMETHING *WAS* HAPPENING THERE

Dayton's took a psychedelic trip on March 4, 1967, when two twenty-four-year-olds, Steven Cohen and Peter Nevard, brought their Fantasy Unlimited to the store to simulate what one might experience if one had taken LSD.

Minneapolis Star columnist Barbara Flanagan asked Cohen and Nevard if their "Sensations '67" show could truly be psychedelic without the hallucinogenic drug.

"Psychedelic is a generic term," Cohen told Flanagan. "Maybe the world of children is psychedelic. Maybe it's what you see when you close your eyes and rub them. It's what you hear and feel. One of the things about taking LSD is that it lets you use 80 percent of your brain when usually you only use 10 percent of it."

Cohen told her that he had taken several LSD trips but had a hard time putting the sensation he'd felt into words. Cohen and his partner were attempting to re-create the experience with lights, music, sounds and images projected from slides and cameras. Nevard told Flanagan that he hadn't had the courage to take an LSD trip yet.

The two men had shot twenty rolls of film inside Dayton's of displays, people, whatever they could see, and then programmed the slides to flash onto the walls of the eighth-floor auditorium along with lights. Models were part of the multimedia experience, which transformed the twelve-thousand-square-foot auditorium into an "environmental envelope" that showered attendees with "1,000 shattered images of light."

People could try it at home, Cohen said, with a hi-fi, strobe lights, slide projectors and movies.[6]

In 1964, Dayton's introduced four mannequins "representing the Negro race" in its window displays. The faces for the mannequins had been modeled after black actresses, including Diahann Carroll. In addition, Wells, who was vice-president of advertising at that time, said the store was also hiring its first black model, New Yorker Bani Yelverton, who modeled in the 1958 Friends of the Institute fashion show fundraiser for the Minneapolis Institute of Arts. Wells, who had worked with fashion photographer Erwin

Blumenfeld on the show, later suggested that Blumenfeld use Yelverton in a fashion shoot for Dayton's Oval Room that appeared in the October 14, 1958 issue of *Look* magazine.

On the management side, the 1960s saw Bruce Dayton become president in 1965. Donald was elected the company's first chairman of the board. Kenneth became executive vice-president and general manager of Dayton's, the posts formerly held by Bruce, and Stuart W. Wells was named vice-president of merchandise and publicity.

In October 1967, the Dayton Corporation went public with its first common stock offering. On March 7, 1969, the *New York Times* reported that Dayton's and the J.L. Hudson Company of Detroit would merge into a new company, the Dayton Hudson Corporation. At the time, Hudson's operated the country's third-largest department store in Detroit, after Macy's Herald Square in Manhattan and Marshall Field's in Chicago.

Hudson's was the largest privately held department store in the United States. The new corporation staged a huge flower show on Wall Street on September 9 to celebrate the Dayton Hudson Corporation's (DHC) listing on the New York Stock Exchange.

Chapter 12

The Family Steps Down and the Minnesota Legislature Saves the Day

The Dayton Hudson Corporation experimented and expanded with jewelry stores, a tire company (Lechmere Tires and Sales), consumer electronics (Team Central) and even a catalogue showroom through the late 1960s and into the '70s. The company bought the Lipman Wolfe department stores in 1968, and by 1979, Dayton Hudson owned stores throughout the United States—Dayton's in Minnesota, North Dakota and South Dakota; Diamond's in Arizona and Nevada; Lipman's in Oregon; J.L. Hudson's in Michigan and Ohio; and the John A. Brown chain in Oklahoma. Target was operating in eleven states.[1]

B. Dalton, Bookseller, started the decade with 27 stores. By 1978, there were 357 in forty-three states, including a flagship store on Fifth Avenue in Manhattan. That same year, Dayton Hudson bought Mervyn's, a midscale department store chain with stores in California, Nevada and Arizona. In Minnesota, Dayton's Home Stores were opened in Edina and in Roseville.

By 1976, the Dayton brothers had stepped down from management positions at the company. Donald, Wallace and Douglas had retired from management and the board of directors by 1978. Their cousin, George Draper Dayton II, retired as vice-president of the Dayton Hudson Corporation in 1972.

Dayton's—what *Minneapolis Star* columnist Jim Klobuchar described as one of three institutions in which Minnesotans had an unbreakable faith (church and the potluck supper were the other two)—was moving into a new era. What defined that for Klobuchar was the day he walked into the Minneapolis store to buy a button for an overcoat.

"There are no buttons here," he was told on a January morning in 1978.

"I'm sorry, Madame, I misunderstood you. For a moment, I thought you were telling me Dayton's doesn't sell buttons," he said to a store clerk.

"We don't sell buttons anymore," was the reply.

Dayton's had always sold buttons. "Never have I walked into Dayton's without my every need being satisfied and a few new ones being identified," Klobuchar wrote.

The end of button sales at the Nicollet Avenue store—which had been there before Social Security or Medicare, before shopping centers or credit cards, the store that had outlasted the League of Nations and the British empire—had just crushed an illusion for the writer: "If you couldn't find it at Dayton's, either it didn't exist or it was illegal."[2]

Bruce and Kenneth Dayton retired from the Dayton Hudson Corporation Board of Directors in 1983, ending eight decades of direct family involvement with the company. Three years later, the corporation sold B. Dalton, Bookseller, to Barnes & Noble.

The change in leadership coincided with changes in Dayton's flagship store, which began with a remodel of the lower level. Ending its reign as a bargain basement, the eighty-three-thousand-square-foot space would be devoted to an "open-air market" that included housewares, gourmet

The 1987 Santabear merchandise. *Dayton Hudson media packet, Hennepin County Library.*

foods, a bakery, a candy shop and an express-service café. The floor also included a pharmacy, a housewares department, a bed-and-bath department and an electronics department. The budget merchandise that was once housed in the lower level was integrated into departments throughout the store. The basement remodel was the first phase of a floor-by-floor remodel of the store.

On the day after Thanksgiving 1985, Dayton's introduced a holiday collectible that lasted more than two decades: Santabear. The conception

101

Santabear and Miss Bear take to the sky in 1987. *Dayton Hudson media packet, Hennepin County Library.*

of Dayton Hudson marketing executive John Pellegrene—who also brought Giorgio and the Boundary Waters brand to the store—the white plush bear wore a red scarf and a cap embroidered with the name "Santabear," and 400,000 of them sold within three days. A new version was introduced each holiday.

In 1987, Miss Bear was introduced, and in 2000, the two bears tied the knot. Miss Bear was dressed in a white gown and veil, and Santabear wore a tux and hat. The two bears sold for $38.50 each, and of course, quantities were limited.

Santabear had stints as a firefighter, a magician, an astronaut and even a father. Collector editions of the family of three went on sale for $175 at Macy's stores in 2007, the year the bears were retired.

A SCULPTURE GARDEN ON THE EIGHTH FLOOR

"Imagine a 100-foot-by-40-foot field of 25,000 tulips shaded in waves from pink to red to purple, interspersed with the sculpture of Noguchi, Marini, Flanagan, and Moore." So began the Dayton Hudson press release announcing the 1988 Dayton's-Bachman's spring flower show, "A Sculpture Garden."

The show was a salute to the opening of the Minneapolis Sculpture Garden, an outdoor art installation that was a project of the Walker Art Center and Minneapolis Park and Recreation Board. The flower show was displayed in the eighth-floor auditorium and drew more than 100,000 visitors.

In addition to the garden show, sculptor Roy Lichtenstein, whose twenty-five-foot sculpture *Salute the Painting* was on

An illustration from the marketing materials for the Dayton's-Bachman's "A Sculpture Garden" from 1988. *Hennepin County Library.*

the front steps of the Walker Art Center at that time, designed an art shopping bag that was used in the store during the flower show. It was the latest in a series of art bags that the Dayton Hudson Corporation, in conjunction with the Walker Art Center, commissioned from contemporary artists for special occasions.

Horse and Rider, by Marino Marini, was shown in "A Sculpture Garden" in 1988. *Hennepin County Library.*

In the fall of 1984, Frank Stella designed a bag to salute the new print galleries at the Walker. David Hockney's 1985 bag honored the British Festival of Minnesota, and Annie Leibovitz's 1985 bag featured her photograph of Dayton Hudson's celebrity Santa, Willard Scott. In 1986, graphic designer Eiko Ishioka created a bag to honor the Walker's Tokyo: Form and Spirit exhibition.

One of the first bags Dayton's designed as an art bag was to honor the Walker's Picasso exhibit. That bag, along with several others, is in the Smithsonian's collection. The Lichtenstein bag was sold for thirty cents in all Dayton's stores during the 1988 show.

A story that made headlines in Minnesota and in major newspapers in New York and Chicago was the 1987 Dayton Hudson takeover attempt by a Maryland company, the Dart Group. It pulled the Minnesota Legislature into a special session to pass one of the country's toughest anti-takeover laws to protect the state's largest employer.

In the spring of 1987, an anonymous investor began acquiring Dayton Hudson stock. By June, shares had soared nearly $6 on heavy volume.

The company soon found out that the Dart Group, a Maryland company that owned discount bookstores and auto supply stores, was attempting a hostile takeover.[3] Herbert Haft, patriarch of the family-run company, was a pharmacist who started a discount drugstore chain in Washington that reached sales of $283 million before he sold it in 1984.

In June 1987, *Fortune* magazine called Haft one of the country's most feared corporate raiders because of the Dart Group's recent run on both Safeway Stores and Supermarkets General. If Dart were able to takeover Dayton Hudson, there were fears that the group would sell off parts of the giant retailer to pay for the deal and cut jobs along the way.

"There was a term in the '80s called 'greenmail,'" said Paul Campbell, whose company, Campbell Research Inc., was a subcontractor for Dayton Hudson at the time. "Companies would make threats—like an elephant faking a charge—that they would take over a company with the unspoken [understanding] that the company would pay [the raiders] a lot of money to go away."

"Who knows what the real intentions were in 1987," Campbell said. "The Haft family made an overture to Dayton Hudson, and it caused gigantic headlines. The Minneapolis and St. Paul papers were in cardiac arrest."

Campbell recalled returning home after a tennis date that June to hear a message to call Dayton Hudson immediately. Shortly after making the call, Campbell got into his car and drove to the corporate offices in the IDS tower in Minneapolis. There, he was told that the corporation needed a survey conducted from a broad cross-section of Minnesotans that measured the attitudes and awareness of citizens from throughout the state about Dayton Hudson and the attempted takeover. The company wanted to use the survey to persuade the governor into calling a special session to pass anti-trust laws that would prevent the takeover.

"The Dayton family had been model corporate citizens for a really long time, so it had a lot of supporters throughout the state of Minnesota," Campbell said. "It was like having evil triumphing over good. If the Haft family were successful in this takeover, all the good stuff would be gone. It would have been like the end of the philanthropic world."

The Hafts were viewed as "bad guys with bad motives."

Still, legislators needed the session to address more than just the Dayton Hudson Corporation. So, Campbell was tasked with conducting a survey to find out what Minnesotans knew about the hostile takeover and Dayton Hudson, as well as how they felt about Minnesota-owned businesses in general.

"They needed [the survey] really fast. Faster than fast," Campbell said. "I sat down and structured a questionnaire—all within two hours." Campbell was able to call in "all his cards" and found people to do the coding and data entry. "We broke it down to men, women, different age groups, [people from the] north, the rich, the suburbs."

Thirty-six hours after Campbell received that phone call at home, the survey was completed. "We issued a nice-looking typed annotated report the next evening. There was a lot of support for the Dayton Hudson Corporation and a lot of opposition to the bad guys," he said. "What the residents wanted wasn't just a sugar cookie tossed to Dayton Hudson, but to do it for all of Minnesota corporations. It was presented to the legislature that Sunday night, and that's all they needed."

Governor Rudy Perpich called a special session, and the Minnesota Legislature—both Republicans and Democrats—joined forces and passed the measure by well more than the required two-thirds majority. The legislation was based on an Indiana law that had recently been upheld by the U.S. Supreme Court, as well as a law in New York.

A key provision of the law made any hostile takeover prohibitively expensive. That provision forbade the sale of any of a target company's assets for five years after the acquisition, which makes it difficult to finance or pay interest on the debt for the bid. The law also forced a raider who acquired 20 percent or more of a company's stock to get approval from a majority of the target firm's shareholders to receive voting rights for its stock. Neither the raider nor the target company's management could participate in that vote. Much of the law was made retroactive to June 1, 1987.

"We'll never know what would have happened if [the legislature had] dilly-dallied," Campbell said. "In that world, dilly-dallying would have been terminal for the company." As for the Hafts, "they kicked their feet up, threatened and got angry, and nothing really came of it," Campbell noted.

Then the stock market collapsed in October.

"Talk about an interesting time," he said. "But just after the stock market collapsed, the Minnesota Twins won the World Series."

Chapter 13

A Century of Dayton's Comes to a Close

Today, many Minnesotans believe that Marshall Field's bought Dayton's department stores in 1990, setting in motion the close of a longstanding institution in the Land of Lakes. But in April 1990, it was the Dayton Hudson Corporation that bought Chicago's leading retailer for nearly $1.4 billion. This made Dayton Hudson one of the largest department store retailers in the nation.

Kenneth Macke, chairman of the corporation at the time, told the press that the company planned to keep all twenty-four Field's stores—from Ohio to Texas—under their current name and continue a $120 million renovation to the downtown Chicago store. Marshall Field's shoppers wouldn't see much change in their stores' selection or presentation of merchandise, he said.

The Marshall Field's purchase came one month after Dayton Hudson announced that it would refurbish the exterior of the Minneapolis Dayton's store, which—no surprise—came at the same time as a renovation of Nicollet Mall.

Dayton's exterior would be restored by stripping six layers of brown paint and putting glass back in the storefront windows. The store used the same color green around the façade of its new windows that George Draper Dayton had used when the building was constructed in 1902. Part of the renovation included the renewal of a two-story granite colonnade that encompasses the building.

"The project…signals the importance of the values and beliefs that this company was founded on," said Marvin Goldstein, chairman and CEO of

This drawing shows what the exterior of Dayton's would look like after the restoration of the brick and windows in 1991. *Hennepin County Library.*

Dayton Hudson at the time, "and it reaffirms the relevance of that history as we approach the next century."

The merging of traditions at the three department stores—Hudson's, Dayton's and Marshall Field's—seemed inevitable. In 1991, Dayton's began sharing its holiday shows with Marshall Field's and Hudson's. Dayton's 1990 show, *Peter Pan*, was staged at Hudson's in Southfield, Michigan, in 1991. That same year, Dayton's 1989 *Cinderella* set filled the windows at Marshall Field's Chicago store.

In 1992 Dayton's announced that it would drop its Spring Oval Room Show in Minneapolis and instead stage *A Cause for Applause*, the Minneapolis version of Hudson's *Fash Bash* in Detroit. *A Cause for Applause* would benefit the Children's Cancer Research Fund and was held in July that year. In 1995, *A Cause for Applause* became known as *Fash Bash*. It branched out to Chicago in 1999 and was renamed *Glamorama* in 2003. Macy's still stages *Glamorama* each spring at the State Theatre in Minneapolis, and it still benefits the Children's Cancer Research Fund.

Dayton's stopped selling major appliances in 1993. At that point, the only stores that sold them were the flagship store in downtown Minneapolis and three Home Stores. The other Dayton's stores had stopped selling appliances eight years earlier.

Dayton's made a bold change in its ninety-year-old liberal return policy in April 1993: Customers who wanted to return merchandise for cash without a receipt had to wait two weeks for a reimbursement check to come in the mail. Charge accounts were credited immediately, however. Customers with receipts would get instant cash refunds. The change was intended to curb shoplifting.

By 2000, Target had become the core business of the Dayton Hudson Corporation, and the company name changed to Target Corporation to reflect that. The next year, the Dayton's name disappeared from the corner of Seventh and Nicollet, at the Dales, and from the stores in other parts of Minnesota and in North Dakota and South Dakota. Target renamed the Dayton's and Hudson's stores Marshall Field's "because it is known worldwide and represents our largest business," said Linda Ahlers, Hudson's, Dayton's and Marshall Field's president and CEO, at the time.

In 2004, Target Corporation sold its Mervyn's chain, and in 2005, Target shed its department store division, selling Marshall Field's to May Department Stores Company for $3.2 billion. In less than a year, Federated Department Stores acquired the May company.

In 2006, all Marshall Field's stores became Macy's.

Chapter 14

Don't Touch the Popovers

M acy's River Room restaurant in downtown St. Paul served its last popover on January 31, 2013. The restaurant, a downtown destination for businesspeople and shoppers since 1947, closed along with the rest of the department store, which had transitioned from Dayton's to Marshall Field's and finally to Macy's in 2006.

The restaurant opened in Schuneman's department store at Sixth and Wabasha in the 1940s. Schuneman's became Dayton's in 1959, and four years later, Dayton's moved the store across the street into its new building at 411 Cedar Street, which was designed by Southdale architect Victor Gruen. The River Room moved with it.

The restaurant went through several renovations while a part of the Dayton's stores. In 1982, the Waterford crystal chandeliers from Dayton's Sky Room restaurant in Minneapolis were brought in. That's about the same time River Room manager Robert Johnston handed a popover recipe to baker Immacolata Colosimo and said, "Try this."[1]

Johnston (aka "Mr. J") brought the recipe from a restaurant he had managed in Rochester, Minnesota, according to Leanne Dobson, a River Room waitress for more than twenty-eight years.

The popovers—which became a Dayton's restaurant staple and are still served in Macy's Minneapolis Oak Grill and Southdale Lakeshore Grill— were the most important thing in the restaurant, said Dobson. "If we ran out of popovers, it was horrible. I heard a story of a new executive chef

The Tiffin was a restaurant on the twelfth floor that was a little more casual (and more mod) than the Sky Room or the Oak Grill. *Hennepin History Museum.*

who said, 'You've had the same bread program for over twenty years, and someone told him, 'You can't touch the popovers.'''

Macy's shared several recipes from the book *Someone's in the Kitchen with Dayton's Marshall Field's Hudson's*, some of which are still being used in Macy's Minnesota restaurants today.

Next page: The Tiffin menu in 1960. *Hennepin History Museum.*

TIFFIN

please check your choice of entree and dessert

entrees

- ☐ Tomato Tower Salad with Chicken Salad on Garden Lettuce, Stuffed Olive Garnish, Crisp Potato Chips, Date Nut Bread and Butter Sandwich
- ☐ Assorted Fruit Plate with Pineapple Sherbet, Mandarin Orange, Honeydew and Plums, Fruit Cream Dressing
- ☐ Baked Stuffed Veal Birds, Veal Gravy, Whipped Potatoes, Gravy, Fresh Corn on the Cob
- ☐ Baked Roast Beef Hash, Fresh Vegetable Relish, Fresh Corn on the Cob, Fresh Tomato Slice

(No Substitutions Please)

desserts

- ☐ Fresh Apple Pie
- ☐ Devils Food Cake, Allegretti Icing
- ☐ Chocolate Chiffon Pie
- ☐ Strawberry Sundae
- ☐ Pineapple Sherbet
- ☐ Fruit Gelatin, Whipped Cream
- ☐ Vanilla or Peppermint Ice Cream

- ☐ Black Coffee
- ☐ Golden Guernsey Milk
- ☐ Coffee with Cream
- ☐ Orange Pekoe Tea

$1.05

Daytons

(No Tipping Please)

8-25-60

In compliance with the President's Food Conservation Plan, Bread or Rolls will be served only on request. No Meats will be served on Tuesdays. No Eggs will be served on Thursdays.

The Dayton Company.

_____

SUGGESTIONS — 75c.

No. 1
Chicken Salad, Bran Muffin

No. 2
Creamed Fruit Salad Served with Tiffin Room Sandwich

No. 3
Creole Spaghetti with Creamed Fresh Mushrooms and Crisp Bacon, Candied Sweet Potato, Buttered New Peas

Devils Food Cake, Chocolate Icing
Peppermint Ice Cream   Date Cream Pie

☆

Boulder Bridge Pasteurized Guernsey Milk, Coffee or Tea

_____

Monday, November 17th, 1947.

The Tiffin menu in 1947. *Hennepin History Museum.*

The Sky Room menu cover, circa 1960. *Hennepin History Museum.*

POPOVERS

Note: Allowing the batter to rest for 15 to 30 minutes before dividing into preheated pans will make for a lighter, more tender popover.

5 eggs (about 1 cup)
1⅔ cups whole milk
5 tablespoon unsalted butter, melted
1⅔ cups flour
½ teaspoon salt

Preheat oven to 400 degrees. Lightly coat popover pans or deep muffin tins with nonstick cooking spray and preheat pans in oven for at least 15 minutes (covering pans with aluminum foil will keep cooking spray from splattering).

In a medium bowl, using an electric mixer on medium-high speed, beat eggs until frothy. Add milk and butter and mix well. Reduce speed to low and add flour and salt, and mix until just combined.

Divide batter among preheated pans, filling each cup just under half full (fill empty cups halfway with water). Bake for 30 to 40 minutes—do not open oven door—until popovers are puffy and brown.

Remove from oven, transfer pans to a wire rack and cool 2 minutes. Popovers should pull away from the pan easily; if not, use a dull-bladed knife to nudge them from the pan. Serve warm.

Makes 12 popovers.

BOUNDARY WATERS SALAD

2½ cups cooked wild rice
1 cup (4 ounces) cooked duck meat, torn into pieces
2 green onions, cut into rings
½ cup mayonnaise
2 tablespoons red wine vinegar
1½ teaspoons Dijon mustard
¼ teaspoon dry mustard
salt and pepper to taste
2 small tomatoes, each cut into 8 wedges
2 small hard-cooked eggs, quartered
½ cup small broccoli flowerets, blanched
4 small mushrooms, halved

Combine the rice, duck and green onion in a mixing bowl. In a small dish, combine the mayonnaise, vinegar, both mustards, salt and pepper. Add to rice mixture and mix well. Chill well before serving. Service the salad garnished with tomato wedges, hard-cooked eggs, broccoli and mushrooms.

Makes 4 servings.

BOUNDARY WATERS WILD RICE SOUP

6 tablespoons butter
1 small yellow onion, chopped
½ cup all-purpose flour
4 cups chicken broth
1 cup whipping cream
⅓ cup dry sherry

1½ cups cooked wild rice
½ teaspoon white pepper
salt to taste

Melt butter in a medium pan. Add onion and cook 5 minutes until soft. Stir in flour and cook 1 minute, stirring often. Add broth and whisk until smooth. Add cream and sherry and heat to a simmer. Add rice, pepper and salt. Simmer gently 5 minutes, just until heated through and slightly thickened. Serve hot.

Makes 6 1-cup servings.

KEY LIME PIE

4 large eggs
½ cup plus 2 tablespoons fresh lime juice
1 can (14 ounces) sweetened condensed milk
1 prebaked 9-inch or 10-inch pie shell
1 cup whipping cream

Preheat oven to 400 degrees. Beat eggs until frothy. Mix in lime juice, then milk, mixing well. Pour into pie shell. Bake until slightly warm, about 7 minutes. Cool to room temperature and then refrigerate several hours before serving. At serving time, beat cream until it holds soft peaks. Spread over top of pie.

Makes 1 pie.

Chapter 15

Retail Legacy

A dozen blocks northeast of the spot where George Draper Dayton opened a department store in 1902, two of his great-great-grandsons have launched their own venture into retail with their men's boutique.

Askov Finlayson is one of three businesses that Eric and Andrew Dayton opened in the Marvel Rack Manufacturing building on North First Street in Minneapolis's North Loop neighborhood. A nod to their boyhood trips to the family cabin on Lake Vermillion, the store got its name from an exit sign seen traveling south on Highway 35 that reads, "Askov Finlayson," two tiny towns straddling both sides of the highway. (The exit sign going north reads, "Finlayson Askov.")

The store was opened in late 2011, just a few months after the brothers opened the Bachelor Farmer restaurant and Marvel Bar in the same building.

Eric and Andrew—grandsons of Bruce B. Dayton and sons of Minnesota governor Mark Dayton—aren't the only Dayton progeny who seem to have inherited the retail bug. Scott Dayton—who grew up with Harold, the fine women's clothing store that Scott's father, Robert, launched in downtown Minneapolis in the 1970s—opened Twill by Scott Dayton in 2004 at the Galleria in Edina. The store is a block from Southdale, the mall that Dayton's grandfather, Donald, and great uncles built. The store describes itself as an "updated traditional gentleman's clothing store" that carries exclusive brands with classic, timeless design.

Scott's brother, James, owner of James Dayton Design Ltd., an architecture firm whose work includes his cousins' restaurant, also designs men's shoes. James Dayton created the Dalton boot for the Allen Edmonds Shoe Corporation, a client of the architecture firm since 2007. (The boot's name is a nod to B. Dalton, Bookseller, the bookstore chain that his family started in the 1960s and derived its name from "Dayton," changing the *y* to an *l*.) Dayton's firm designed the Allen Edmonds store in Minneapolis City Center, just across the skyway from the old Dayton's store.

Is the bent toward retail genetic? Eric Dayton said no. "I can assure you that we don't have any inherent magical genetic retail gift that makes us master retailers," he said. Although Eric went to business school at Stanford and worked for eighteen months at Target before going to graduate school, he said that he and Andrew have had to "start from zero and make our way and learn as we went, like anybody else starting in this business."

The North Loop area of Minneapolis is an up-and-coming neighborhood with more retail and residential developments moving in. Similar to the decisions their great-great-grandfather made more than a century ago, Eric and Andrew Dayton chose to open businesses in a location that's not central to downtown but is an area fast being developed.

While he acknowledged that many Minnesotans feel a sense of loss with the closing of his family's department store business, Eric Dayton noted a positive change in retail in the Twin Cities.

"More and more small retailers are starting to pop up in Minneapolis and St. Paul, where before there weren't a lot of unique shops," he said. "There seems to be more of a returning appreciation for things made in America, where there's a story behind the product and it's not just a commodity at the lowest price."

The appreciation of quality and greater values being placed on locally owned businesses is something that people might not have valued when they had it but miss now, he said.

The days of getting everything one needs under one roof may be ending, but the value placed on local businesses seems to be resurging.

Notes

Chapter 1

1. Dayton, with Green, *George Draper Dayton*, 58.
2. Ibid., 67.
3. Ibid., 205.
4. Dayton, with Green, *George Draper Dayton*, 69.
5. Ibid., 211.
6. *Minneapolis Journal*, May 23, 1903.

Chapter 2

1. *Minneapolis Journal*, June 25, 1902.
2. Dayton, with Green, *George Draper Dayton*, 247.
3. Ibid., 250.
4. Ibid.
5. *Daily News*, "Tea Rooms Opened in Dayton's Store," August 1, 1906.
6. Dayton, with Green, *George Draper Dayton*, 261.
7. Firestone, *Dayton's Department Store*, 22.
8. *Minneapolis Journal*, March 9, 1909.
9. Dayton, with Green, *George Draper Dayton*, 267.

Chapter 3

1. *Minneapolis Tribune*, "Dayton Company Buys Property on Eighth Street to Insure Facilities," August 10, 1916.
2. Gray, *You Can Get It at Dayton's*, 69–70.

3. Dayton, with Green, *George Draper Dayton*, 282.

4. *Minneapolis Tribune*, "Fire Will Hasten Plan to Enlarge Big Dayton Store," February 18, 1917.

5. Gray, *You Can Get It at Dayton's*, 91.

6. Dayton, with Green, *George Draper Dayton*, 275.

7. Dayton, with Green, *George Draper Dayton*, 285.

Chapter 4

1. Gray, *You Can Get It at Dayton's*, 80.

2. *Minneapolis Sunday Tribune*, "Twentieth Anniversary of Dayton Store Proves Faith of Founder," February 5, 1922.

Chapter 5

1. Dayton, with Green, *George Draper Dayton*, 300.

2. Ibid., 302.

3. Ibid., 305.

4. Ibid., 311.

Chapter 6

1. Gray, *You Can Get It at Dayton's*, 164.

2. Tselos, George, *Self-Help and Sauerkraut*, 307–8.

3. Gray, *You Can Get It at Dayton's*, 170.

4. *Minneapolis Journal*, "I'll Do My Part" advertisement, November 30, 1933.

5. Dayton, with Green, *George Draper Dayton*, 506–7.

6. *Minneapolis Tribune*, February 19, 1938.

Chapter 7

1. Gray, *You Can Get It at Dayton's*, 255.

2. Ibid.

3. Ibid., 257.

Chapter 8

1. Barbara Flanagan, *Minneapolis Tribune*, date unknown.

2. Dayton, with Green, *Birth of Target*, 46.

CHAPTER 9

1. Dayton, with Green, *Birth of Target*, 35.
2. Cline, *Vera Way Marghab Story*, 173.
3. Dayton, with Green, *Birth of Target*, 40–41.
4. Rowley, *On Target*, 112.

CHAPTER 10

1. Marling, *Merry Christmas!*, 97.

CHAPTER 11

1. Dayton, with Green, *Birth of Target*, 56.
2. Martin Merrick, "Dayton's Aide Tells Retailers to 'Swing Well with Young,'" *Minneapolis Star*, October 11, 1966.
3. Mike Steele, "Dayton's Opens Russian Art Show," *Minneapolis Tribune*, June 4, 1967.
4. Firestone, *Dayton's Department Store*, 101.
5. *Minneapolis Tribune*, June 21, 1968.
6. Barbara Flanagan, "It's a 'Happening,'" *Minneapolis Star*, March 3, 1967.

CHAPTER 12

1. Dayton, with Green, *Birth of Target*, 74.
2. Jim Klobuchar, "One of His Illusions Crashes at Dayton's," *Minneapolis Star*, January 31, 1979.
3. Rowley, *On Target*, 163.

CHAPTER 14

1. Gail Rosenblum, "River Room's Retired Popover Princess Looks Forward to Spaghetti," *Star Tribune*, February 28, 2013.

Bibliography

Bergerson, Roger. *Winging It at a Country Crossroads: The Ups and Downs of Minnesota's First Real Airport: Snelling and Larpenteur, Rose Township 1919–1930*. St. Paul, MN: Bergerson & Cunningham, 2008.

Cline, D.J. *The Vera Way Marghab Story*. Brookings: South Dakota Art Museum, 1998.

Dayton, Bruce B., with Ellen B. Green. *The Birth of Target*. Minneapolis, MN: privately published, 2008.

———. *George Draper Dayton: A Man of Parts*. Minneapolis, MN: privately printed, 1997.

Dayton Hudson Corporation. *Someone's in the Kitchen with Dayton's Marshall Field's Hudson's*. Minneapolis, MN: Dayton Hudson Corporation, 1992.

Firestone, Mary. *Dayton's Department Store*. Chicago, IL: Arcadia Publishing, 2007.

Gray, James. *You Can Get It at Dayton's*. Minneapolis, MN: privately published, 1962.

Marling, Karal Ann. *Merry Christmas! Celebrating America's Greatest Holiday*. Cambridge, MA: Harvard University Press, 2001.

Minneapolis St. Paul Magazine. "The Goldstein Presents: Fashion Lives Fashion Lives." August 2000.

Pitrone, Jean Maddern. *Hudson's: Hub of America's Heartland*. West Bloomfield, MI: Altwerger and Mandel Publishing Company, 1991.

Rowley, Laura. *On Target: How the World's Hottest Retailer Hit a Bull's-Eye*. Hoboken, NJ: John Wiley & Sons Inc., 2003.

Saporito, Bill, and Edward C. Baig. "The Most Feared Family in Retailing." *Fortune*, June 22, 1987.

Tselos, George. "Self-Help and Sauerkraut, The Organized Unemployed Inc. of Minneapolis." *Minnesota History* (Winter 1977). Published by the Minnesota Historical Society, St. Paul, Minnesota.

Index

About the Author

K ristal Leebrick lives in St. Paul, Minnesota, where she is the editor of a nonprofit monthly community newspaper and writes for several publications.